Positive

A play by Shaun Kitchener

Published by Playdead Press 2015

© Shaun Kitchener 2015

Shaun Kitchener has asserted his rights under the
Copyright, Design and Patents Act, 1988, to be
identified as the author of this work.

A CIP catalogue record for this book is available from
the British Library.

ISBN 978-1-910067-37-6

Printed by BPUK

Playdead Press
www.playdeadpress.com

Ann Pinnington Productions
in association with **West Avenue** presents

Positive

By Shaun Kitchener

CAST (in order of appearance)

Benji	**Timothy George**
Nikki	**Nathalie Barclay**
Greg	**Paul Heelis**
Olly	**Ryan J Brown**
Jennifer	**Claire Greenway**
Margo	**Sally George**
Matt	**Shaun Kitchener**

Director	**Harry Burton**
Designer	**Marcio Santarosa**
Lighting Designer	**Nic Farman**
Sound Designer	**Andy Hinton**
Stage Manager	**Sarah Rhodes-Cannings**

Producer	**Ann Pinnington**
General Manager	**Chris Corner**
Press & Marketing	**Target Live**

This production of *Positive* was performed at Park Theatre
7 July - 1 August 2015

*This text went to press before the end of rehearsals
and so may differ slightly from the play as
performed.*

Shaun Kitchener | Writer & 'Matt'

Positive is Shaun's first full-length play. One-act productions include *Caravan*, *It Never Rains* (both White Bear Theatre) and *One Night Stand* (Edinburgh Fringe), while various shorts have been staged at London theatres including Waterloo East, Rosemary Branch, Hen & Chickens and Bread & Roses. Shaun is a former member of the Royal Court Young Writers' Programme and the Soho Theatre Writers' Lab. He was also nominated for the 2014 Offie Award for Most Promising New Playwright. Journalism includes V.Point, Telegraph, Mirror, Holy Moly! and EntertainmentWise; and he also produces, writes for and acts in the regular scratch night Briefs via his theatre company, West Avenue. Other acting includes *Christmas Monologues* (Bread & Roses), *Soggy Brass* (Hen & Chickens), *One Night Stand*, *Chamber Music* (both Edinburgh Fringe) and *Big Love* (Union Chapel, Norwich).

Harry Burton | Director

Harry trained as an actor at Central and as a director with BBC TV. Directing credits include *The Dumb Waiter* (Trafalgar Studios), *Quartermaine's Terms* (Tour), *I Found My Horn* (Chichester & Trafalgar Studios), *The Leisure Society* (Trafalgar Studios), *Casualties* (Park 90), *Barking in Essex* (Wyndham's) and *Parzival* (Sharpham House). He is about to direct Harold Pinter's *Ashes To Ashes*, starring Dame Harriet Walter, for BBC Radio. Harry has directed two films: *Thinspiration* (Channel 4) and *Working With Pinter* (Channel 4).

Ann Pinnington | Producer

Ann Pinnington was Associate Director/Producer at the New End Theatre London where she produced many plays including *From The Hart*. She was Co-Artistic Director at the Kings Head Theatre, working on many of their productions including *Cavalcade, You Can't Take it With You, Stairway to Heaven, Pageant, Ghosts, Journey's End* and many more. She was Director of Theatre Royal Presentations, Bath and HCS Productions London, and worked extensively with Portman Theatrical Productions who produced 64 number one tours including *Killing of Sister George* with Beryl Reid, *The Winslow Boy* with Marius Goring and the first production of *The Seven Year Itch*. Many of these transferred to the West End including the acclaimed production of *Jungle Book* and the award winning *When We Are Married*. Her overseas work includes Off Broadway and Aspen Festival productions. Recently she produced two plays by Anton Burge at the Arts Theatre: *A Storm In A Flower Vase* and the acclaimed *Bette and Joan* starring Anita Dobson and Greta Scacchi, which subsequently toured the UK in association with Mark Goucher. She has just co-produced the touring stage version of *The Kings Speech* starring Jason Donavan.

Marcio Andrey Santarosa | Designer

A Set and Costume Designer who recently graduated from Wimbledon College of Arts/ University of Arts London.

Recent credits include *The Picture Of Dorian Gray*, *The Dead Shepherd* (both White Bear Theatre), *Strangers Welcome* (Tabard Theatre) and *Overture*, a festival of short musicals at Tristan Bates Theatre, in collaboration with Goldsmiths University.

Nic Farman | Lighting Designer

Credits include *Shock Treatment* (Kings Head), *Daisy Pulls it Off*, *A Level Playing Field* (both Shoreditch Town Hall), *The Heart of Things* (Jermyn Street), *Dracula!* (Soho), *Pig Girl, Valley of Song, The Immortal Hour, Hostage Song, (*Finborough*) Empires* (Bush), *Lysistrata, Romeo and Juliet, Still the Beating of my Heart, Blood Wedding, Mac-Beth, Last of the Red Hot Lovers, The Woyzeck* (Tour), *Richard III* (Cockpit, Greenwich), *Little Mermaid* (Riverside), *The Bald Prima Donna, The Upstanding Member, The Blind/The Intruder* (Old Red Lion), *Cinderella* (Leicester Square), *Fulfil Me Fully, Phil, A Life in Monochrome* (The Space) and *The Laramie Project* (Leicester Curve).

Andy Hinton | Sound Designer

Design credits include *Sweeney Todd* (Twickenham Theatre), *Armstrong's War* (Finborough), *The Cat's Mother* (Courtyard, Hoxton), *The Light In The Piazza, Hello Again, The Last Five Years, Yerma, Fire Island, Trojan Barbie* (Mountview), *Hairspray, Noises Off, Crazy for You, Kiss Me Kate, In The Club, The Drowsy Chaperone* and *The Producers* (Shrewsbury Theatre Severn). Non-design credits include *The Wind in the Willows* (Vaudeville), *Buddy: The Buddy Holly Story* (Tour); *Midsummer Night's Dream* (Stafford

Festival Shakespeare), *Hands on a Hardbody, Snoopy!: The Musical, Legally Blonde, Twang!!* (Guildford School of Acting), *The Hired Man, Besame Mucho, Scenes from the Heroic Life of the Middle Classes, Rent, #boundforglory2013 Flashmob* (Mountview).

Christopher Corner | General Manager
A freelance theatre company administrator and production manager for over 20 years, Chris has managed productions for many of the major new writing companies including Foco Novo, Joint Stock, Bristol Express, Paines Plough, Bright Red, Moving Theatre, The Half Moon, Lifeblood Theatre and Opera Machine. Also work with York Early Music Festival, Leicester Haymarket, Sheffield Crucible, Royal Court and the Royal Opera House. He project manages The Wrestling School, a company that tours the work of Howard Barker in Europe. He is currently general managing work for Kali Theatre, Yellow Earth Theatre, Sean Graham Dance and Andy Jordan Productions.

Nathalie Barclay | 'Nikki'
Trained at Mountview Academy. Credits include *Much Ado About Nothing* (New Wimbledon Theatre Studio), *Consolation* (Théâtre Volière), *Positive* (Waterloo East Theatre & Edinburgh Fringe), *A Gaggle of Saints* (The Albany*)*, *The Boy Who Never Learned To Fly* (Arcola

Theatre), *Indian Summer* (White Bear Theatre), *Breaking News* (Cockpit Theatre), *Macbeth* (Lion and Unicorn Theatre), *Grotto* (Old Red Lion). *You Once Said Yes* (Nuffield Theatre) and *Fire Island* (Charing Cross Theatre). Film credits include: *Awakening* (Canted Image Productions), *Gradulthood* (Will Hall-Smith), *50 Year Valentine* (EmJay Productions).

Ryan J Brown | 'Olly'

Trained at Goldsmiths U.O.L and Mountview. Recent theatre credits include *Buttery Brown Monk* (Leicester Square Theatre), *Games of Love and Chance* (Edinburgh /London), *Caravan* (White Bear Theatre), *Briefs* (Rosemary Branch /Waterloo East Theatre), *Plunge* (Theatre Deli), *Positive* (Waterloo East Theatre), *Anna Karenina* (Camden), *The Dispute* (The Bridewell), *Rainman* (Karamel, London) and *Hamlet (Mountview)*. Film credits include *Sherlock Holmes 2: A Game of Shadows*. He is also a writer and has trained with the BBC. Several of his plays have been performed at The Royal Academy of Dramatic Art.

Sally George | 'Margo'

Trained at Guildhall. MA at Central School of Speech and Drama. Spent several years with the RSC. Credits there include *Richard III* (Australia), *Merry Wives, Titus Andronicus, Penny for A Song, Misalliance, Taming of the Shrew* (UK & Japan) *The New Inn, Fashion, Oedipus* (Almeida), created role of Maggie in Vaclav Havel's *Temptation*. Other theatre: *When We Are Married* (UK tour), *Comedy of Errors, The Jolly Potters* (New Victoria Stoke). *Something Blue* (Stephen Joseph Scarborough), *House And Garden* (Theatre Royal Northampton), One woman shows *My Matisse & A Case Of The Poet* played New End Hampstead, Edinburgh Festival, Dylan Thomas Festival and UK tours. TV & film includes: *The Buddha of Suburbia, Persuasion, Measure for Measure, Women At War, Death of Romance, Mulberry, Daziel and Pascoe*. Radio: *The Roy Orbison Story, Rock and Roll, King Street Juniors, Richard III* and *Temptation*. Recently completed *Love Somehow*, a film about Caitlin Thomas, playing Caitlin (wife of Dylan). She will be in *Roaring Trade* at the Park later this year.

Timothy George | 'Benji'

Trained at Mountview Academy of Theatre Arts. Prior to this, graduated from the University of Manchester with a First Class Honours degree in Drama & English Literature. Theatre includes *The Woman in the Moon* (Rose Playhouse), *Positive* (Edinburgh Fringe/Waterloo East Theatre), *The Comedy of Oedipus* (Lion & Unicorn Theatre), *Medea* (Guildhall Art Gallery), *Fire Island* (Charing Cross Theatre), *Spring Awakening* (Salford Arts Theatre) and *The Shadow Master* (King's Head). Film and TV includes *Amundsen* (BBC), *The 11 O'Clock Show* (Channel 4) and *Persuasion* (BBC). Timothy also holds an MA in Theatre for Young Audiences from Rose Bruford.

Claire Greenway | 'Jennifer'

Trained at Royal Academy of Music. Originated the role of Sister Mary Patrick in *Sister Act* at the London Palladium, performing at the Royal Variety Performance and in many TV appearances. Other theatre includes *Therese Raquin* (Finborough and Park). *James and the Giant Peach* (Birmingham Stage), *Cinderella, Sleeping Beauty* (Stafford Gatehouse), *Betwixt!, Spinach* (Kings Head), *Cinderella* (Epsom Playhouse), *Richard Bucket Overflows, Hot Mikado*

and *Miss Sign-On*. TV and film includes *Phoneshop*, *Little Crackers*, and *Anna Karenina*. Other credits include *Monkey – Journey to the West* (O2), singing backing for Elton John and several movie soundtracks including *Transformers*, *Sweeney Todd* and *Pirates of the Caribbean*.

Paul Heelis | 'Greg'

Paul graduated from Mountview Academy of Theatre Arts in 2013. Since leaving he has been a regular performer with West Avenue, appearing in many of their quarterly scratch nights and this year performing in the double bill *Caravan/Pin* at The White Bear Theatre. Other recent credits include *Mahr* (The Cockpit Theatre), *Daves* (Above The Arts Theatre), *The Office Christmas Party* (Theatre Delicatessen) and short film *Wasted*. Paul has been playing the role of Greg since *Positive* began as a rehearsed reading and is delighted to still be involved in this new production.

Park Theatre is a theatre for London today. Our vision is to become a nationally and internationally recognised powerhouse of theatre.

★★★★★ *"A spanking new five-star neighbourhood theatre."*
Independent

We opened in May 2013 and stand proudly at the heart of our diverse Finsbury Park community. With two theatres, a rehearsal and workshop space plus an all-day cafe bar, our mission is to be a welcoming and vibrant destination for all.

We choose plays based on how they make us feel: presenting classics through to new writing, musicals to experimental theatre, all united by strong narrative drive and emotional content.

Alongside a large number of world premieres - including *Daytona*, with Maureen Lipman, which toured nationally and transferred to the West End - and UK premieres - including *Yellow Face*, which transferred to the National Theatre Shed, we have presented thrilling first revivals such as Richard Bean's *Toast*, with Matthew Kelly.

★★★★★ *"Constantly compelling."* Daily Telegraph on *Toast*

We have welcomed over two hundred thousand visitors through our doors, but as we grow we're looking forward to developing our audience base, reaching out into the community locally, forging partnerships internationally and continuing to attract the best talent in the industry.

To succeed in all of this, ongoing support is of paramount importance. As a charity with no public subsidy, none of this is possible without the help of our Friends, trusts and foundations and corporate sponsors. To find out more about Park Theatre, our artistic and creative learning programmes and how you can support, please go to **parktheatre.co.uk**

'NOBODY DIES': THE WRITER'S INTRODUCTION

I was on a train home from work in December 2012 when I got the idea for Positive. I was reading a magazine column by a guy in his twenties, talking about his love and social lives and how they were affected by his positive HIV status.

I realised that most representations of the virus on film and on stage are gloomy tales of sickness and tragedy, but that's not what it's like in real life anymore - at least not in our part of the world. In fact, the more people I spoke to, the more I realised that nowadays it's stigma, anxiety and depression that can be the hardest hurdles for HIV+ people to overcome; often more so than the HIV itself. With that in mind, I wanted something upbeat, warm, honest and up-to-date. Something in which, crucially, nobody is ever in danger of being killed off.

It feels like a lifetime ago that the play's first draft was put up in front of a tiny audience in Camden as a rehearsed reading. March 3, 2013, to be exact; after which it headed up to Edinburgh on the most shoestringy of shoestrings and was fortunate enough to pull in enough unanimously strong reviews to convince me to take it further.

After a lot of redevelopment and redrafting, it then ran at London's Waterloo East Theatre in May 2014; giving me one of the best experiences of my life – as both a writer and an actor. Again, our budget was practically non-existent; but with a fantastic company we gathered more support, more (pun alert) positive feedback and I for one learned a huge amount about so many aspects of theatre-making.

Now, 31 months after that first train journey, I'm so excited that Positive has arrived at one of my absolute favourite venues. I'm still lapping up what continues to be an incredible experience, and massively grateful to everyone who helped it get here.

Oh, and as a side-note: bonus points for anyone who spots the pattern in the characters' surnames...

Shaun Kitchener, playwright

ACKNOWLEDGEMENTS

The writer would like to thank:

- Ann Pinnington for believing in the play and enabling it to continue its journey. I am so grateful for this experience and will never forget it.

- All who helped inform and inspire the script, especially Tom Hayes of Beyond Positive for putting up with my initial base-level questions!

- Actors Timothy and Sally George, Nathalie Barclay, Paul Heelis and Ryan J Brown for staying aboard for as long as two-and-a-half years; making the show better and better with every outing.

- Claire Greenway, Chris Corner, Marcio Santarosa, Nic Farman, Andy Hinton, Sarah Rhodes-Cannings, everyone at Park Theatre and of course the almighty Harry Burton for investing so much talent, time and energy into the play and really shifting it up a gear for this production.

- All the talented actors, directors and producers from past incarnations of *Positive* – James Callas Ball, Alice Wright, Rob Ellis, Will Marsh, Lorna Baillie, Natalie Lester, Katherine Edrupt, Marc Gee-Finch and Edward McLean - without whom there's no way we'd be here now. Thanks especially to Jamie-Rose Monk for not only being an A+

actor but also for all the help and encouragement since day one (and for letting us put soup in your hair in Edinburgh).

- Everyone who has helped along the way: Robert Morris and the team at Silver Jubilee Park, Stephen Davies, Clemmie Hill and Andrew Greer at Target Live, Gerald Armin at Waterloo East and anyone who has helped us in any way whatsoever over the last couple of years. That includes you, Britney.

- Finally a big, personal 'cheers' to Nick Bentley and the Kitchener family (Mooz, Cheex, Obes and Scoob) for being consistently above average in the love and support department, and for seeing the play approximately 485 times. I'd offer to reimburse all the ticket and travel costs, but...

Characters, in order of appearance:

BENJI, 26. *Keeps on keeping on. A happy person who's not quite himself.*

NIKKI, 27. *Pragmatic over-thinker. Better at helping others than herself.*

GREG, 30. *Kind-hearted nice guy stuck in the wrong job in the wrong country.*

OLLY, 19. *Fun-loving student, ignorant to the world, not ready to grow up.*

JENNIFER, 30s. *Sexual health physician. Professional, caring, exemplary.*

MARGO, 50s. *Conservative middle-class parent trying to open her mind.*

MATT, 27. *Blunt and direct on the surface, with genuine warmth.*

Notes on the text:

A forward slash (/) indicates a point of interruption.
An *italicised phrase* within dialogue indicates emphasis.
[*Square brackets*] within dialogue contain stage directions.

ACT ONE

Today. Monday morning. A London flat: comfortable if unspectacular.

Somewhere off-stage, a shower is on.

BENJI enters from outside. He's looked better. He's wearing the same clothes he wore the night before, including a fairly smart shirt.

Careful not to make too much of a sound, he takes his shoes and jacket off.

The shower stops.

BENJI drops his keys and flinches.

NIKKI: [*Off*] Benji?

No reply.

             Benji, is that you?

BENJI: Yep.

NIKKI enters, dressing gown on, straight from the shower. Face like thunder.

NIKKI: What the *fuck?*

BENJI: Morning.

21

Positive

NIKKI: Don't 'morning' me, you bastard, where were you?

BENJI: What do you mean?

NIKKI: Do you have any idea how worried we were?

BENJI: My phone died.

NIKKI: We know that; we spent all night trying to bloody ring it!

BENJI: I was out.

NIKKI: Where?

BENJI: Nowhere special.

NIKKI: You can't just vanish for a whole night and expect me not to worry.

BENJI: Are you done in the shower?

NIKKI: Benji…

BENJI: I've got my appointment.

NIKKI: Where were you?

BENJI: Just out! What's the problem?

NIKKI: You've barely left the flat for the last God-knows-how-long, you can't / just expect me to –

BENJI: I was at a bar, OK?

Beat.

NIKKI: A bar?

BENJI: Yes.

NIKKI: What bar?

BENJI: Somewhere central.

NIKKI: What were you doing in a bar?

BENJI: Am I not allowed?

NIKKI: You haven't been near one for the entire time I've known you.

BENJI shrugs.

Who'd you go with?

BENJI: Friends.

NIKKI: What friends?

BENJI: From work!

NIKKI: Really?

BENJI: You're starting to sound like my mum.

NIKKI: I was just worried, that's all.

BENJI: Well I'm a grown adult. I'm not 15.

NIKKI: Hey, come on. I worry about you. You haven't been out in ages and then suddenly you disappear / unannounced –

BENJI: I didn't disappear. I'm all right! I'm good. Thank you.

Beat.

NIKKI: I mean the least you could have done was invite me along.

BENJI laughs a little.

And you owe Greg an apology.

BENJI: How come?

NIKKI: It was our one-year anniversary, remember? Poor guy was expecting all the sex but I was too busy thinking about you.

BENJI: Urgh.

NIKKI: Not like that.

BENJI: I need to get ready…

NIKKI: What time's your appointment?

BENJI: Ten.

NIKKI: Ten? It's barely eight! Come on, you went out! You *socialised*! This is big news; you're lucky I'm not hanging up the bunting.

BENJI: All right, patronising...

NIKKI: No, not patronising, just... pleasantly surprised.

GREG enters from elsewhere in the flat; suited up and ready for work.

GREG: Morning.

NIKKI: Look who's here!

GREG: I heard, you little bastard!

NIKKI: And guess who had a wild night out?

GREG: Really? Fuck off!

BENJI: Why is everyone so shocked?

NIKKI: He's been moping around for, like, what, a year? No social life, no drinking, no *fun*, dare I say it, apart from what he gets up to in the privacy of his own room...

GREG: Oi oi!

BENJI: Oh come on...

NIKKI: And then he sneaks in at 8am after a big spontaneous bender and wonders why we're a tiny bit interested.

GREG: Didn't know you had any friends, mate.

BENJI: Well I do!

NIKKI: People from work, apparently.

GREG: Ah.

BENJI: I really need a shower...

NIKKI: Tough, I used all the hot water. You'll have to wait half an hour.

BENJI: Fuck's sake.

GREG: I've got to go. Glad you're OK, Benj.

BENJI: I'm fine!

GREG kisses NIKKI goodbye.

GREG: And you – let me know if you hear anything.

NIKKI: I will.

GREG: Here we go. Another day in hell!

BENJI: Bye.

NIKKI: See you.

GREG leaves.

BENJI: You think you're gonna find out today?

NIKKI: Don't you change the subject. This isn't over!

BENJI: I'm just asking…

NIKKI: Your mum rang me last night, by the way.

BENJI: Why?

NIKKI: She was worried; you weren't answering her calls.

BENJI: What did you tell her?

NIKKI: I feel terrible, I lied! I made something up; told her you were at work.

BENJI: Thanks.

NIKKI: Only 'cause I didn't want to worry her. You need to call her back.

BENJI: I know what it's about. She wants to come and visit. Sort everything out.

NIKKI: And that's bad because…

BENJI: I can't be bothered.

NIKKI: Can you at least let her know you're alive? I don't like lying for you.

BENJI: I'll do it tonight.

NIKKI remembers something.

NIKKI: Oh, shit, tonight…

BENJI: What?

NIKKI: Don't have any plans, do you?

BENJI: No…?

NIKKI: Good. Don't make any.

BENJI: Why not?

NIKKI: Because I've got something for you…

BENJI: What is it?

NIKKI: A hot date.

BENJI: Sorry?

NIKKI: You're welcome!

BENJI: Wait, you've… What?

NIKKI: Before we realised you'd buggered off, I got Greg to text that mate of his and ask if he was up for it, and he said yes, so we / asked him when he's free…

BENJI: Absolutely not, no way.

NIKKI: Why not?

BENJI: I'm good, thanks.

NIKKI: This has been on the cards for weeks, you can't back out now!

BENJI: I was never backed *in*!

NIKKI: But Greg's already told him you'd –
You've got love-bites on your neck.

BENJI: Huh?

NIKKI: You've got – what are they called – hickeys!

BENJI: Oh. Ow. Yeah.

NIKKI: Where did they come from…?

BENJI: Nowhere.

NIKKI: Where did you sleep last night?

BENJI: I didn't.

NIKKI: *What?*

BENJI: It's not what you think!

NIKKI: Shitting hell, Benji!

BENJI: I mean it!

NIKKI: This is too good… I'm going to get dressed and put the kettle on, and then you're going to tell me absolutely everything. OK?

BENJI: I already have!

NIKKI: *OK?*

BENJI: Nikki! What do you want me to say?

NIKKI: Two minutes. Don't move. I want every detail.

NIKKI exits.

The scene changes.

The night before. Smoking area outside a nightclub.

Music can be heard, as if from inside.

BENJI is idly standing, as if taking a breather. Playing around on his phone.

OLLY arrives, a little tipsy. He takes out a cigarette. Notices BENJI.

OLLY: Busy.

BENJI: Huh?

OLLY: Busy out here. Little joke.

BENJI: Oh, yeah! Rammed.

OLLY: Having a good night?

BENJI: Yeah, great, thanks.

OLLY: Got a light?

BENJI: No, sorry, I don't smoke.

OLLY: Just hanging out in the smoking area...

Beat.

I'd ask if you come here often, but...

BENJI: Am I that obvious?

OLLY: I think it's the shirt. Very smart.

BENJI: It's new.

OLLY: Fresh from the packet, I can see the creases.

BENJI: Oh...

BENJI blushes, slightly embarrassed.

OLLY: Bit full-on in there, isn't it.

BENJI: A bit.

OLLY: What's your name?

BENJI: Benji.

OLLY: What's that?

Positive

BENJI: Benji.

OLLY: I'm gonna call you Ben. I'm Olly.

BENJI: All right.

OLLY: You must be freezing.

BENJI: I'm OK.

OLLY: Alcohol blanket?

BENJI: Sleeves.

OLLY: Ah! Where are your friends?

BENJI: Inside.

OLLY: Not keeping you entertained?

BENJI: They're fine. Just really drunk.

OLLY: At least they're here! Mine are all massive let-downs, going on about deadlines and lectures and all that...

BENJI: Lectures?

OLLY: They take it all so seriously.

BENJI: You're a student?

OLLY: Yeah! Like anyone else is out on a Sunday. Apart from sad old people.

He laughs. BENJI doesn't.

You're not a student, are you...

BENJI: No.

OLLY: Sorry. It's all right! I love older guys!

BENJI: Thanks...?

OLLY: You're really cute.

BENJI: Oh... no...

OLLY: Definitely.

BENJI: Thanks.

Beat.

OLLY: So I've got a bit of a dilemma.

BENJI: Yeah?

OLLY: A conunder – conundrum? Can't even say it.

BENJI: OK...

OLLY: You know when you're like a *bit* drunk, and you could either nip it in the bud and go home or just get properly smashed?

BENJI: Yeah?

OLLY: That's me.

BENJI: Right.

OLLY: What do you reckon?

BENJI: Me?

OLLY: You gonna let me buy you a drink? Or do I need to run for the last tube?

BENJI: Um…

OLLY: Don't be nervous!

BENJI: I'm not.

OLLY: Well then. Let's turn that thing off…

He helps himself to BENJI's phone and switches it off.

And get some more creases on that shirt. Deal?

Beat.

BENJI: OK.

OLLY: Let's go.

OLLY makes his way back inside. BENJI follows and then stops, hesitant.

You all right?

BENJI: Yeah.

OLLY: Well…

OLLY & JENNIFER:
                  Come on then.

BENJI: Yeah.

JENNIFER: Benji. Benji!

OLLY: What are you waiting for?

Music subsides as OLLY exits and the scene changes.

Today. Consultation room at a GP surgery.

JENNIFER is waiting.

JENNIFER: Hello? Earth to Benji…

BENJI: Hmm?

JENNIFER: Come on!

BENJI: Come on what?

JENNIFER: Are you gonna sit down?

BENJI: Oh! Yeah.

JENNIFER: I'm not talking for my health here.

BENJI: Sorry.

JENNIFER: For *your* health, yeah? Not for…
Forget it. How's it going?

BENJI: Fine.

JENNIFER: Any problems?

BENJI: Not that I can think of.

JENNIFER: Sleeping any better?

BENJI: About the same. Late nights, late mornings.

JENNIFER: Right.

BENJI: Don't.

JENNIFER: I didn't say anything.

BENJI: It's my job! It's fucked up my body clock.

JENNIFER: Your job?

BENJI: Yeah! It's not a 9-5 thing. I'm on air at all hours.

JENNIFER: Oh, do me a favour.

BENJI: I am!

JENNIFER: You're not 'on the air'! The DJ whose producer's assistant you're interning for is 'on the air'.

BENJI: It's just 'on air' / actually…

JENNIFER: Secondly, it's not all hours. It's late afternoon, and it's three times a week. I know, all right, I tuned in the other day.

BENJI: Really?

JENNIFER: Yes. Lovely segment on single over 30s.

BENJI: I did the research for that.

JENNIFER: Thirdly, the reason you aren't sleeping any better is because you've let yourself get into this rut. *Again.* Why won't you go and see the counsellor like I keep suggesting?

BENJI: I went to that support group, didn't I?

JENNIFER: A few times, but it was a long time ago.

BENJI: And my test results are spotless.

JENNIFER: I haven't told you them yet.

BENJI: Well they usually are. Aren't they?

JENNIFER: Yeah, they're… they're fine. But that's not the point, and you know that's not the point.

Beat.

BENJI: How am I doing?

JENNIFER: Fine. Good. Viral load's still undetectable, CD4's up to 548. STI check's all clear.

BENJI: See? I'm great.

JENNIFER: How's the rash?

BENJI: Starting to fade.

JENNIFER: About time it buggered off. Still causing irritation?

BENJI: Something like that.

JENNIFER: Meaning?

BENJI: It's fine.

JENNIFER: Good. Well it seems like, medically speaking, everything's still on the right track. Remember to check in at reception; make sure your meds are replenished.

JENNIFER gives him an envelope containing his results and prescription, which he takes.

BENJI: I will.

JENNIFER: But listen, I have homework for you.

BENJI: Homework?

JENNIFER: Homework. We're gonna stick in your next appointment for a few months' time, and in the meantime I want you to promise me you'll make a serious effort to... get a life.

BENJI: What?

JENNIFER: You heard. Try and get out of the house for something other than work and medical appointments. Meet a friend for lunch, go on a night out... Have some drinks, I don't care, as long as you don't get too carried away.

BENJI: I'm actually way ahead of you.

JENNIFER: What do you mean?

BENJI: I mean I went out last night.

JENNIFER: Oh really...

BENJI: Really.

JENNIFER: To what, take the bins out?

BENJI: No...

JENNIFER: Corner shop? Did you buy a pint of milk?

BENJI: No! I went out; I went out-out.

JENNIFER: Seriously?

BENJI: Yes!

JENNIFER: Oh. Well. That's a first.

BENJI: You look as surprised as Nikki was.

JENNIFER: You weren't with her?

BENJI: I have other friends! Why is everyone so stunned?

JENNIFER: No, yeah, sure, I was just... wow. You'll be telling me you're having casual sex next! I'm glad you got out. Let off some steam.

BENJI: Thank you. Do I get a lollipop? Or a sticker?

JENNIFER: Nope, that's the dentist.

BENJI: Dentist, sexual health consultant. Same difference.

JENNIFER: All yanking and prodding, isn't it. Well it sounds like we *are* making good progress after all. Did you have fun?

BENJI: Uh – yeah, yeah.

JENNIFER: Good. I know you hate my prying and it's technically not my job to pester you about your social life...

BENJI: "Technically."

JENNIFER: But I care about you. You know that. Why else would I put myself through those stupid Britney CDs?

BENJI: Oh, that reminds me! I bought the next one.

JENNIFER: Great...

BENJI: The education continues.

JENNIFER: I hope I'm gonna get some extra letters after my name for this.

BENJI produces a Britney Spears CD with the sleeve notes missing.

BENJI: OK, this one is Circus. Not one of her best, if you ask me, but there are a couple of tunes on there. That's the Deluxe Edition, by the way – the bonus DVD is definitely worth a watch.

JENNIFER: And is this post-meltdown or pre-meltdown?

BENJI: Post-meltdown. Remember that last one I gave you was the one where she was just this fabulous hot mess...?

JENNIFER: Right, yeah, I'm with you. Where's the booklet thing?

BENJI: It folds out into a poster.

JENNIFER: Of course it does. If you were half as enthusiastic about anything else as you are about Britney Spears, we wouldn't have a problem.

BENJI: We don't have a problem.

JENNIFER: Good. Come on, I'll walk you out. Don't suppose you have any chewing gum?

BENJI: Think so. Do you need some?

JENNIFER: No, but you do. I can smell the vodka from here.

BENJI: Ha ha.

They leave.

The scene changes.

Later the same day. Back at NIKKI and BENJI's flat.

NIKKI is on the phone. Anxious.

NIKKI: Hi, it's Nikki Harding, I was just –
Harding? H – A – R – D – I… Great.
I was just expecting a call at some point today – well, before today, really – about my application to…
Yeah, yeah, and I'm just ringing to see if there's any news at all?
Sure, no, that's fine.

Elsewhere, simultaneously, MARGO is also on the phone.

MARGO: Benjamin, this is your mother. For the fiftieth time. I have just received your text message. All three words of it. Can you call

42

me back? Please? You know I'd set today aside to come down and see you; it's very frustrating when you won't talk to me properly. Give me a call and we'll sort out another time. We haven't had the chance to talk since last time you were here; you can't just leave it all up in the air like this.

I thought I might take you to the Rainforest Café. Will that do it...? Anyway, call me. Please.

She hangs up and exits.

NIKKI: Really? How later is later?

No, I know, I understand... I just, my boyfriend is...

Yeah. Of course. Thank you anyway. Just let me know as soon as you can.

All right. Bye.

She hangs up and GREG enters.

GREG: Anything?

NIKKI: No.

GREG: That sucks.

NIKKI: They said 'later'.

GREG: What, today?

NIKKI: Today, this week, this month...

GREG: That's annoying.

NIKKI: I'm so sorry, I was / really hoping to –

GREG: Don't worry about it! It's cool.

NIKKI: How was work?

GREG: I cannot wait to be out of there. I swear it's actually getting worse.

NIKKI: Not long now.

GREG: Yeah.

Beat.

Hey, Matt's all set for tonight. Raring to go!

NIKKI: Oh, shit, I didn't text you...

GREG: Text me what?

NIKKI: Benji's not going.

GREG: What? You're kidding.

NIKKI: I mentioned it to him this morning and he completely blew it off.

GREG: I thought he was keen!

NIKKI: Me too!

GREG: It's half six now! Matt'll be on his way.

Positive

NIKKI: What do we do?

GREG: I'll have to text him. Tell him to go home again.

NIKKI: I'm sorry.

GREG: It's not your fault. What is wrong with that guy?

NIKKI: Benji? He's just... He's depressed. Not that he'll admit it.

GREG: Then surely it'd do him good to get out? Meet someone?

NIKKI: I can't force him.

BENJI enters.

GREG: What a moron.

NIKKI: Speaking of whom...

BENJI: Who's a moron?

NIKKI: You.

BENJI: What? Why?

NIKKI: It's nothing, it's my fault. Kind of.

BENJI: What is?

NIKKI: I told you this morning; that Matt guy was up for meeting you and I forgot to tell Greg to cancel it.

BENJI: Well that was stupid.

GREG: He's going to be so pissed off with me.

NIKKI: Oh, no, tell him it was my fault. I don't mind.

GREG: I don't want him being angry with you.

NIKKI: It's fine!

BENJI: Oh, please.

NIKKI: What?

BENJI: I see what's going on here.

NIKKI looks at him blankly.

You didn't tell him on purpose and now you're going to tell me I *have* to go so he doesn't feel like he's been stood up.

NIKKI: No, but… If that's how you feel…

BENJI: Nikki!

NIKKI: It's just one date, nobody's asking you to get married!

GREG: Am I texting him or not?

BENJI: Yes! Do it.

NIKKI: No, hang on a second...

BENJI: But I'm *so* tired...

NIKKI: Benji, it's been over a year! You need to get that love life back on the move! And anyway, Greg said he's really nice, didn't you?

GREG: I didn't say *that*...

NIKKI: Well we're saying it now. Come on, what's the big deal? Why are you so against a bit of spontaneity?

BENJI: I'm not against spontaneity; I just don't like it being sprung on me.

NIKKI: Will you please just go? For me!

BENJI: No! Look, thank you for the offer and I promise I'll think about meeting him some other time. But tonight I'm just going to stay in and watch Crossroads.

NIKKI: Fuck's sake, Britney is not the answer to everything!

BENJI: That's a lie and you know it.

NIKKI: OK, you know what... fine. Fine. Have it your way.

GREG: So shall I tell him you're not going?

BENJI: Yes. Please.

Unseen by BENJI, NIKKI indicates otherwise to GREG.

NIKKI: Right then, let's get some food in, shall we? All three of us? That'll be nice.

BENJI: If you want.

NIKKI: Oh, shit... no it's four of us, isn't it?

GREG: Is it?

BENJI: Oh God, please don't ask him to come here...

NIKKI: No, no, not Matt –

BENJI: Who then?

NIKKI: Your mum!

BENJI: What?

NIKKI: Your mum's coming, isn't she?

BENJI: Since when?

NIKKI: She texted me earlier, saying she'd rung you or something, and she'd see us all tonight...? No?

BENJI: I didn't speak to her.

NIKKI: Really?

BENJI: Well, she left me a voicemail, but... Are you sure?

NIKKI: Oh shit, maybe I wasn't supposed to say anything... Christ, don't tell her I told you. [*To GREG*] She's really scary.

BENJI: What do I do?

NIKKI: She's only your mum.

BENJI: But we're not speaking!

NIKKI: Perfect chance to sort it out.

BENJI: Did you reply to her?

NIKKI: I could have said anything, she said she was coming anyway. I think she knows you keep trying to sack her off. It'll be fine!

BENJI: No, no it won't be fine.

NIKKI: Why not?

BENJI: I've already told you, she's just – she's – no! I can't see her. I can't. No way. I'd rather die.

GREG: How scary is this woman?

Beat. NIKKI plays her ace.

NIKKI: You know what you *could* do, right? To get out of seeing her?

BENJI: What?

Beat.

Oh, look how that turned out.

NIKKI: Look, personally, I don't see why you can't spend a bit of time with your mum, especially as she's making the effort to come all the way down and see you...

BENJI: I told her I'm busy every night! She'll know I was lying.

NIKKI: ...*However*, if for some reason you wanted to dodge her...

There'll be a guy waiting to have dinner with you at a lovely little Italian restaurant near Tottenham Court Road in just under an hour.

Beat.

You don't have to sleep with him. You don't have to drink. You don't even have to stay for dessert. And I'd like it if you went. I know you had a random night on the lash last night but I hate seeing you all mopey and... lonely.

BENJI: I'm not lonely.

NIKKI: Yes, you are. And I think it'll do you good to have a nice civilised dinner with someone; someone aside from me or him.

BENJI: Does he know?

NIKKI: Know what?

BENJI: About... you know.

GREG: I haven't told him.

BENJI: What's he like?

GREG: He's all right.

BENJI: What time's my mum getting here?

NIKKI: She didn't say.

Beat.

BENJI: Fine. Fine, fine, fine. But you will owe me big for this, yeah? Like... like huge amounts.

NIKKI: Yes!

BENJI: I'll change my shirt.

NIKKI: And your shoes?

BENJI: What's wrong with these?

NIKKI: They just... they look a bit cheap.

BENJI: Well they weren't!

NIKKI: They were £6.99, I bought the same ones for Greg.

GREG: Good pair.

Nice touch if BENJI and GREG are wearing the same shoes.

BENJI: [*Exiting*] I can't believe I'm doing this.

NIKKI: You'll thank me later!

She high-fives GREG.

Man, I'm good.

GREG: Fear of the mother. Works every time.

NIKKI and GREG kiss. She interrupts the moment to check her phone.

Don't worry about Head Office, yeah? They'll call you when they call you.

NIKKI: Yeah, yeah, I know.

GREG: Whatever happens, we'll deal with it. We'll figure it out.

NIKKI: They would have let me know by now.

GREG: You don't know that.

NIKKI: Come on, you're off in like three weeks. They're cutting it a bit fine, don't you think?

GREG: You know what they're like. They'd be stupid to lose you. You were the best they had!

NIKKI: We were the best. We were a great team.

GREG: We are a great team.

Beat. BENJI returns.

BENJI: I'm off, then.

NIKKI: You didn't change your shoes!

BENJI: You need to pick your battles.

GREG: I'll text you the address.

NIKKI: OK, be chatty, yeah? Make lots of conversation.

BENJI: I'm not an idiot.

NIKKI: And be funny! Make loads of jokes, you're really funny when you want to be.

BENJI: I'll tell him the one about the housemate who ruined my evening.

GREG: Ha! That's a good one.

NIKKI: It'll be fine! And hey, even if it isn't - what's that saying you taught me? "If Britney can get through 2007, / then I..."

BENJI: "Then I can get through today." Yeah, we'll see.

BENJI exits.

NIKKI: [*Calling after him*] It's gonna be electric! I can feel it!

She turns to GREG.

Please tell me this guy's gonna be worth it.

GREG looks worried.

Oh, shit.

The scene changes. NIKKI and GREG exit.

That night. A restaurant.

MATT and BENJI are siting, looking at menus, not talking.

After what feels like forever...

MATT: So have we run out of conversation already, or...?

BENJI: What?

MATT: It's been seven minutes.

BENJI: No, no, sorry, I'm just… not really with it today.

MATT: Oh?

BENJI: Yeah, long story.

MATT: I was worried you were nervous or something.

BENJI: Nervous?

MATT: Yeah!

BENJI: Well… a bit, I guess.

MATT: Really?

BENJI: Are you not nervous?

MATT: Oh God, no.

BENJI: …cool.

MATT: There's nothing to lose, is there? If you don't like me or I don't like you, then fuck it.

BENJI: True…

MATT: We don't ever have to see each-other again, so…

Beat.

BENJI: What if Nikki and Greg got married?

MATT: Sorry?

BENJI: If Nikki and Greg got married, we'd probably see each-other at the wedding.

MATT: Good point...

BENJI: Or if they had a massive birthday party or something. Housewarming.

MATT: Yeah, yeah, that's true. Yeah. Or if they died.

BENJI: What?

MATT: If one of them died, we'd probably see each-other at the funeral.

BENJI: Uh... maybe...

MATT: Well if *Greg* died, anyway. I don't really know Nikki well enough to go to hers, if I'm honest. I'd probably feel a bit awkward.

BENJI: Right.

MATT: No offence to her.

BENJI: Of course -

MATT: Obviously if they both died, then I would.

BENJI: Obviously -

MATT: You know, like, plane crash, car crash, natural disaster, something like that.

BENJI: Yeah. Well touch-wood that isn't going to happen, eh?

MATT: Yeah! Oh yeah, yeah, of course... I just meant, you know, if tonight flopped, it'd be a bit awkward if we / then saw each-other...

BENJI: That'd be the main issue at their funeral, yeah.

Beat.

MATT: Sorry... Sorry, I'm a bit... what's the word...

BENJI: Socially inept?

MATT: I'm perfectly... ept! I'm just, sometimes, I'm... a bit...

BENJI: Direct?

MATT: Exactly. Why not just call a spade a spade, and then / you can get on with –

BENJI: And speculate on the possibility of your friends dying young!

MATT: All right! All right, fine. I'll try and behave myself. Try to be... *sophisticated.*

BENJI: Really?

MATT: Nah. Can't be arsed... At least when I say something, you'll know I mean it.

BENJI: Right.

MATT: Like... OK, you might get offended if I told you I wouldn't be caught dead in those frankly offensive shoes, *but* then you'd know I meant it if I said... I don't know... You have *gorgeous* eyes. Wow.

BENJI: Thanks.

MATT: You're welcome.

Beat. Brief moment of intimacy. Then...

See? It works.

BENJI: I like these shoes.

MATT: Well each to their own.

BENJI: What are you having?

MATT: I don't know. I've been staring at the menu for the last five minutes; I don't think I've actually read it. And the service...!

BENJI: Sounds like you're nervous.

MATT: Easy.

BENJI: I'll probably just play it safe. Spag bol, maybe.

MATT: Really?

BENJI: What?

MATT: Uh… no! Nothing…

BENJI: What is it?

MATT: Sorry, no, forget it…

BENJI: What? Why shouldn't I get it?

MATT: You should! Ignore me, knock yourself out, / get that spag…

BENJI: What happened to Mr Cut-To-The-Chase?

MATT: Oh, come on! It's the worst possible thing you could get on a first date, isn't it?

BENJI: What?

MATT: Of course it is! You do want me to find you attractive, don't you? You want me to find you irresistible?

BENJI: I don't know. Do I?

MATT: Of course you do. So imagine my horror and disgust when I look up from carefully cutting up my… I don't know… *swordfish*, and there's you with a bunch of spaghetti dangling out your gob, trying to suck it all in in the sexiest way you possibly can. Urgh! No thank you.

BENJI: Fine, I'll just have a pizza.

MATT: Oh, don't be so weak.

BENJI: What?

MATT: Weak! Don't be such a pushover! Stand by your decisions; don't let anyone else's opinion get to you...

BENJI: What do you want me to have?

MATT: Bollocks does it matter what I want you to have. I'm paying for it, / you may as well get whatever you can take...

BENJI: But you *just* said that... Wait, *paying* for it?

MATT: Course.

BENJI: Why?

MATT: Because I want to.

Beat.

Because I like you.

BENJI: Oh.

MATT: And I'm impressed that you haven't walked out by now.

BENJI: You're really hard to figure out.

MATT: Yeah, I'm an enigma. It's part of my appeal.

BENJI: Right.

Beat.

MATT: So what's the baggage?

BENJI: What?

MATT: The baggage, come on. Let's just get it all out in the open.

BENJI: What... now?

MATT: Yeah! Better I find out about your creepy ex now than in a couple of weeks when he stabs me down a back alley. Not a euphemism.

BENJI: I don't have a creepy ex.

MATT: Sure?

BENJI: Yeah.

MATT: Excellent. That's good.

Beat.

I do, FYI.

BENJI: Really?

MATT: Yeah. Not a murderer! Not yet, anyway.

BENJI: Well... good, I guess.

MATT: Just, you know... clingy. Had to change my number. That sort of thing.

BENJI: Oh no.

MATT: Yeah, awful. *Awful.* Really bad. And I mean all right, full disclosure, his dad had *just* died, so I can see how he was a *bit* needy, / but like, get a grip, you know what I mean –

BENJI: Oh God...! Poor guy!

Beat.

MATT: Oh yeah! Yeah, obviously, terrible, really, really sad. Really sad. I just meant... you know...
I didn't walk out on him, or anything, not while he was... I wouldn't have... We were never that big of a thing, not officially, I just meant...

Beat.

OK, I should probably... Rewind! I was a bit late to the whole 'Gay Thing', actually, and when I was first... exploring... I explored with him. This guy I met on that creepy iPhone app... what's it called… You know the one, where everyone's like 'Hey, I'm two feet away, wanna bum?'

BENJI: Yeah.

MATT: Like, 'here's a picture my dick, fancy it?'

BENJI: I know the one.

MATT: And after a few weeks he wanted to make it properly official, and like, I hadn't even decided I was a full on pole smoker by that point, so… That had to be that.

BENJI: Wow.

MATT: If I'd have known his dad was inches from death, obviously I wouldn't have… I don't want you to think I'm insensitive.

BENJI: I'm more concerned by 'pole smoker', to be honest.

MATT: Well that's my creepy ex, anyway. Sort-of-ex, at least.

BENJI: Thank you for sharing.

MATT: Anytime! I need a drink…

He looks for a waiter.

Anyone…?

No luck.

Positive

All right. Now you go.

BENJI: What?

MATT: It's your turn!

BENJI: I don't think so.

MATT: Why not?

BENJI: I'm not comfortable with this on a first date!

MATT: Oh, come off it.

BENJI: You can't throw the rulebook at me over spaghetti bolognaise and then expect me to start talking about my exes.

MATT: I get it. I get it. Your stories must be really bad.

BENJI: That's not what I meant!

MATT: Let me guess, you... You fell for an old guy?

BENJI: No.

MATT: Teacher?

BENJI: No.

MATT: *Relative?*

BENJI: No!

MATT: Hmm. You perplex me. I am perplexed.

BENJI: Now who's the enigma?

MATT: Status change. Interesting.

BENJI: If you're so comfortable, why don't you just tell me about another one of yours?

MATT: Exes? Only got one other. Not a lot to say, really. Serial cheater, standard fare.

BENJI: That's nasty.

MATT: Yep. I mean his arse had more people in it than... fucking... Gatwick... but let's not talk about that.

BENJI: I'm sorry.

MATT: Don't be.

BENJI: Must have hurt.

MATT: Yeah, well...! It's fine. When life gives you lemons, you make lemonade, right? Move on! Try and find someone who isn't going to drag you through hell and back.

Beat.

You must have *something*.

BENJI: What?

MATT: Come on! I just bared my soul. I gave you one demon ex-boyfriend and one clingy fuck buddy, and you've got nothing?

BENJI: I can't think of anything.

MATT: Bullshit.

BENJI: I'm not that interesting!

MATT: Come on!

Beat.

BENJI: Actually, there is... There is something I should probably just put out there. I wasn't going to say anything 'cause I wasn't sure if... I don't know, really, I mean I didn't *not* / want to...

MATT: What is it?

BENJI: I, erm... OK, it's a long story, but... Basically, all right, I...

MATT laughs a little, in something of a daze.

What?

MATT: What?

BENJI: What is it?

MATT: Nothing... no, sorry...

BENJI: What?

MATT: Carry on, sorry, you were saying –

BENJI: Have I got something on my...?

MATT: No! No...

BENJI: I don't get it.

MATT: There's nothing to get!

BENJI: What is it?

MATT: Nothing! No, I was just... I was just *observing*...

Beat.

You're adorable. Really, really adorable.

Long beat. MATT is embarrassed.

Where are the waiters in this place?

MATT and BENJI exit.

Later that night. Back at NIKKI and BENJI's flat.

NIKKI is on the phone. Again.

NIKKI: Hi, it's Nikki Harding, I'm just returning a call from...

It's really not that hard to... H-A-R-D-I...
Thanks.
Yeah, I missed a call from you about ten
minutes ago. I was just chasing it up?
Thank you.

Beat.

Hi. Yep.
Really? Shit...
Yeah! Yeah, that's great news, I'm really...
thank you.
OK, yeah. I'll keep an eye out. Have you
got my email... awesome.
Yep, no issues. Everything I sent you is
still... nothing's changed.
Great! Thank you again. I'll be in touch.
Thanks! Bye.

BENJI enters from elsewhere in the flat.

BENJI: All right?

NIKKI: Didn't wake you, did I?

BENJI: Oh please, you know my body clock!
What's going on?

NIKKI: I got the call.

BENJI: It's half eleven!

NIKKI: Think they knew I was tearing my hair out.

BENJI: And?

Positive

NIKKI: Looks like I'm going back.

BENJI: Oh my God!

NIKKI: I can't believe it.

BENJI: Congratulations.

NIKKI: Greg'll be happy.

BENJI: And you?

NIKKI: Yeah, of course!

BENJI: When are you off?

NIKKI: Like three weeks.

BENJI: That's soon.

NIKKI: I know, right?

BENJI: You OK?

NIKKI: Yeah! After last time... the amount I cost them in medical bills... I didn't think they'd take me back.

BENJI: It's great news.

NIKKI: Yeah.

Beat.

Sorry, how was tonight? How did it go?

BENJI: Yeah, fine! Don't worry about me...

NIKKI: Do you like him?

BENJI: He's quite something.

NIKKI: Is that good?

BENJI: Maybe.

Beat.

Are you gonna call Greg?

NIKKI: He'll be in bed now. I'll tell him tomorrow.

BENJI: I'm really happy for you.

NIKKI: Thanks. So, are you seeing him again?

BENJI: Potentially. We're texting.

NIKKI: Love it.

BENJI: I'd forgotten how stressful it is.

NIKKI: Texting?

BENJI: Yeah! All those rules about leaving it a certain amount of time so you don't look too keen, knowing how many kisses to put...

NIKKI: Fuck it, just text him straight back!

BENJI: Nah. I'm quite enjoying it.

NIKKI: Well. Who'd have thought you'd end up having a good time? Oh wait. I did.

BENJI: It probably won't come to anything.

NIKKI: Why not?

BENJI shrugs.

Did you tell him?

BENJI: No. It's quite a hard thing to just shoe-horn in, you know?

NIKKI: You're overthinking it. He's gonna be fine.

BENJI: You don't know him.

NIKKI: Nor do you, really.

BENJI: He'll probably go off me before it even comes up. Save us both some hassle.

Beat.

NIKKI: Are you gonna be all right? When I go?

BENJI: Yeah, of course I am.

NIKKI gives him a doubtful look.

I'll be fine!

NIKKI:	Of all the positive people I know, you have one of the easiest rides, you know that? On the medical side, I mean. Caught it early, treatment's been fine... people would kill for that.
BENJI:	It hasn't been *that* easy.
NIKKI:	Oh, please. One pill a day? My dad takes more than that for his IBS.
BENJI:	You won't be saying that if I die from lactic acidosis.
NIKKI:	What the fuck is that?
BENJI:	Just one of the many deadly side effects of the prescription / I'm on –
NIKKI:	Oh, bore off! You got a poxy rash for a bit and that's it. And yet still, out of everyone I know, everyone from the support group you've *stopped going to*, you are the one who's struggled most with it. Up here.

She taps her head.

BENJI:	I'm not *that* bad.
NIKKI:	Right...
BENJI:	I went out last night!
NIKKI:	I know.

BENJI: *And* I went on a date tonight. I need reigning in, if anything.

Beat.

NIKKI: Look, about that. I have a confession.

BENJI: What?

NIKKI: You know I said about your mum dropping in?

BENJI: Yeah.

NIKKI: I made it up. I lied!

BENJI: What?

NIKKI: She was never coming down.

BENJI: I knew it!

NIKKI: I just wanted you to go and meet Matt! We've been trying – Greg and I – to get you two set up for ages. Ages! And he's so nice, isn't he?

BENJI: He said he wouldn't go to your funeral.

NIKKI: What?

BENJI: He – never mind.

NIKKI: OK...

Beat.

> But at the risk of repeating myself, I do think you should talk to her. Properly.

BENJI: You need to drop it.

NIKKI: I know you don't get along like a house on fire, but / she seems like she's really trying–

BENJI: You don't know her like I do. Just trust me on this one.

Beat.

NIKKI: Hadn't you better text the old ball and chain?

BENJI: The what?

NIKKI: I think you've left it long enough.

BENJI: Yeah.

NIKKI: I'm gonna try and get some sleep.

BENJI: All right. Congratulations on the Africa thing. I mean it.

NIKKI: Night!

BENJI: Night.

NIKKI exits. BENJI looks at his phone again and, a smile on his face, replies to a message from MATT.

Positive

He picks up a pot of pills. As he's opening them, he's reminded of his situation: what the pills represent and what they're there for. The smile fades.

The scene changes.

The night before. OLLY's flat.

OLLY appears as high-camp pop music suddenly blasts.

Since they met, OLLY has got slightly more drunk. Nerves have sobered

BENJI up a bit, but he's no less keen to be there.

OLLY: So this is my flat! What do you think?

BENJI: It's nice.

OLLY: Do you like this song?

OLLY is dancing; trying embarrassingly hard to be seductive.

BENJI: It's all right.

OLLY: I like it. It's my first-year jam.

BENJI: Wow.

OLLY: Come and dance with me!

BENJI: Dance?

OLLY: Yeah! Come on, loosen up, get those hips going!

BENJI: The night bus really sobered me up –

OLLY: Drink! You need drink.

BENJI: I'm fine, honestly.

OLLY: Will the shop still be open?

BENJI: It's half four, I don't think so..

OLLY: It's cold out there anyway.

BENJI: Yeah.

OLLY: But in here... In here it's *hot*.

BENJI: Oh... right...

OLLY kisses BENJI; gently at first. BENJI takes a couple of beats to ease into it.

OLLY: Mmmm. You taste like dreams.

OLLY kisses him again, now turning up the heat. He tries to remove BENJI's shirt in the process, but due to issues with buttons it's proving more fiddly than anticipated. In the end, OLLY just tries to yank it over his head.

BENJI: Ow, ow, sorry – the – the buttons are – that's my neck. Sorry, let me just...

OLLY momentarily relents while BENJI takes the shirt off himself.

OLLY: Oh, wow.

BENJI: What?

OLLY: Oh *wow*.

BENJI: What is it?

OLLY: Nice body!

BENJI: It's really quite average.

OLLY notices a rash on BENJI's torso.

OLLY: What's that?

BENJI: What?

OLLY: This weird skin bit.

He touches it.

BENJI: Oh - nothing, no, it's – just a weird thing.

OLLY: A birthmark?

BENJI: No, not really –

OLLY: I have a birthmark.

BENJI: Yeah?

OLLY: Next to my penis.

BENJI: Oh – great –

OLLY: Wanna see it?

BENJI: Sure, I – now?

OLLY: So cute!

OLLY goes in for more kissing. This time he grabs BENJI's hands and tries to use them to take his own top off.

Ooh, Beppe, what are you like?!

BENJI: It's Benji, and you've got control of my hands...

OLLY: Shh, Beppe, don't say another word.

BENJI: Benji!

OLLY: Huh?

BENJI: It's Benji, my name's Benji. Not Beppe.

OLLY: Oh. Sorry.

BENJI: That's OK.

OLLY: I'm just so into you, you know?

BENJI: Ah, well –

OLLY: I knew when our eyes first met across that smoking area that we'd end up here.

BENJI: That's very sweet.

OLLY: And then we spoke and I heard your voice for the first time, and... and that smell!

BENJI: It was fun, wasn't it…

OLLY: It was a million tiny little things that, when you added them all up, they meant we were supposed to be together. And I knew it, I knew it the very first time I touched you. It was like coming home, only to / no home I'd ever –

BENJI: Wait, is that… Is that from Sleepless In Seattle?

OLLY: Hmm?

BENJI: I think that's… That's Tom Hanks's big speech in Sleepless In Seattle.

OLLY: No! Is it?

BENJI: I mean it's nice, it's sweet.

OLLY: That's so weird!

Sorry… I'm just… I'm a little drunk.

BENJI: No kidding.

OLLY: Embarrassing…

BENJI: No! No, don't be embarrassed. It's cute. I like it.

OLLY: Yeah?

BENJI: Yeah.

OLLY: 'Cause you know I'm also just a girl. Standing in front of a boy. Asking him to / love her...

BENJI: Notting Hill!

OLLY: You are good at films!

BENJI: They're quite famous speeches...

OLLY: I'm a film student. I *study* them.

BENJI: Oh yeah?

OLLY: Yeah.
You really do have one super-hot bod.

BENJI: Oh... thanks. You too.

OLLY: I thank you!

Beat.

You want to take this upstairs?

BENJI: Yeah...?

OLLY: I'd really like to... just... Yeah.

BENJI: OK.

OLLY: Let's go.

BENJI: Do you have a condom?

OLLY: A what?

BENJI: A condom.

OLLY: What about them?

BENJI: Do you have one?

OLLY: Er… probably?

BENJI: Do you think we should…?

OLLY: Oh yeah, of course, yeah. Definitely. God, you just never know these days, do you? Don't worry, though! For the record, I'm clean! Nothing dodgy over here.

BENJI: OK.

OLLY: Won't catch anything from me!

BENJI: Still, though, I –

OLLY: Relax.

OLLY kisses BENJI.

I'll be really gentle.

OLLY kisses him again. If there's one thing he's not, it's gentle.

Fuck upstairs. Let's do it here.

He takes his jeans off with more difficulty than expected.

BENJI: Woah…

OLLY: I don't wanna waste another second, you… you God.

BENJI: God?

OLLY: Yeah, *sex* God!

OLLY gets back to the kissing, regardless of where he's at with taking his jeans off.

BENJI: Olly, Olly, wait.

OLLY: What is it?

BENJI: About the condom…

OLLY: In a minute.

BENJI: I'd really feel better if we / just –

OLLY: It's fine!

BENJI: No, Olly, please…

OLLY: Look, I'm gonna be honest, yeah? I have no idea where my condoms are.

BENJI: Right.

OLLY: But I promise I don't have anything.

BENJI: Have you ever been tested?

OLLY: No!

BENJI: How do you know you haven't got anything?

OLLY: I think I'd know if I had, like, a rotting ball or something. Come on, you don't see me interrogating you.

BENJI: Well maybe you should!

OLLY: Sorry for trusting you!

BENJI: It's not about that...

OLLY: Benny, just... chill out, yeah?

BENJI: Benji!

OLLY: I'm not gonna hurt you. I promise.

BENJI: I know, but –

OLLY: Now where were we...

He kisses BENJI again.

BENJI: Olly!

OLLY: Jesus, what?

BENJI: There is absolutely no way I'm going any further without a condom.

OLLY: What, do you think I've got chlamydia / or something?

BENJI: I'm HIV-positive.

Beat.

OLLY: You what?

BENJI: I'm HIV-positive. That's what I'm trying to tell you.

OLLY: Are you serious?

BENJI: I just think we should have a condom before we... continue.

OLLY: Oh, shit.

BENJI: Olly –

OLLY: Oh *shit*...!

BENJI: It's all right, it's not a big deal / or anything–

OLLY: I kissed you...!

BENJI: So?

OLLY: But like, I *properly* kissed you!

BENJI: That doesn't matter.

OLLY: And I was literally *just* about to – *fuck*! I'm gonna be sick -

OLLY, getting hysterical, begins wretching.

BENJI: Hey, come on, stop it, you really / don't need to worry –

OLLY: My uncle told me I'd get AIDS!

BENJI: You can't just *get* AIDS.

OLLY: Oh, it all ends the same! And I touched your fucking AIDS rash!

BENJI: AIDS rash?!

OLLY: You know this is illegal, right? To know you're infected and spread it around?

BENJI: This is getting out of hand -

OLLY: You took advantage of me!

BENJI: Look, Olly, I'm sorry I didn't tell you but I never would have let you do anything risky without protection, all right, even though the chances of you catching it anyway would / have been *tiny* –

OLLY: And if I'd got a condom, you still would have told me, yeah?

BENJI: Probably.

OLLY: Oh my God, you weren't, were you?

BENJI: You don't know that.

OLLY: Give me a fucking break, you weren't gonna say a word! You were just gonna let me dip my perfectly healthy carrot into your... hummus of death!

BENJI: If we'd had a condom, it wouldn't have mattered.

OLLY: Don't think it's worth a heads-up? 'Oh by the way, if this breaks, it's curtains for the both of us...'

BENJI: OK, that's enough.

OLLY: Excuse me?

BENJI: Where's my shirt?

OLLY: On top of *my* shirt, which I guess I'm going to have to burn now, you bitch.

BENJI: You need to get some perspective.

OLLY: Perspective? Are you insane? I just had a near death experience!

BENJI: You didn't even want a condom!

OLLY: That's not the point!

BENJI: Of course it's the fucking point! Two minutes ago, you were the one who wanted to go all the way with someone you'd *just met* without any protection whatsoever!

OLLY: You can't spin this on me!

BENJI: And then along comes a guy who insists on being safe so you *don't* catch anything and – oh! – suddenly it's like Christmas Day on EastEnders.

OLLY: This is unbelievable. You know what?

BENJI: What?

OLLY: You know what?

BENJI: What?

OLLY: *You know what?*

BENJI: Jesus, what?

OLLY: We are not having sex anymore.

BENJI: No kidding.

OLLY: I was gonna give you the night of your life.

BENJI: If you say so.

OLLY: You wouldn't have been able to sit down for weeks.

BENJI: That's disgusting.

OLLY: *You're* disgusting. And you're fucking twisted if you think you can get away with shit like this.

                    I'm gonna be sick. I want you gone.

OLLY darts off-stage.

BENJI: Olly, I... Olly, wait...

The scene changes back.

Back at NIKKI and BENJI's flat, as before.

BENJI picks up the pills again, and angrily throws them across the room.

Stressed, he sits down.

A text arrives on his phone. MATT has replied. BENJI smiles at it, then drops his phone down beside him; frustrated with himself.

BENJI: Idiot.

He stares at the thrown pill bottle for a moment, then gets up and retrieves it.

He removes the lid, takes out a tablet and swallows it dry.

End of Act One.

ACT TWO

Two weeks later. A different flat (GREG's). Evening.

NIKKI is sifting through a box of tat, including a lot of old paperwork. There's one sheet in particular that has caught her attention.

After a moment Greg enters with a suitcase.

GREG: Here we are.

NIKKI: Oh, perfect.

GREG: Yeah?

NIKKI: Yeah, that'll be great.

GREG: Save buying a new one.

NIKKI: Are you not gonna need it?

GREG: I packed ages ago!

NIKKI: Ah, this'd save me so much hassle. The amount you have to pay for a good case is ridiculous.

GREG: All right getting it back to yours?

NIKKI: Yeah, I'll just cram it on the tube in the morning. Piss off some commuters.

GREG: Staying here tonight?

NIKKI: Benji invited Matt over, they're having a romantic night in.

GREG: Oi oi!

NIKKI: If one thing leads to another, I might see him in the morning.

GREG: Blimey!

NIKKI: Although Benji's adamant it'll be completely innocent.

GREG: Has he told him yet?

NIKKI: No.

GREG: It's been a fortnight.

NIKKI: I keep telling him the longer he leaves it, the more of a thing it'll be.

GREG: Well, yeah.

NIKKI looks at the suitcase.

NIKKI: It's quite big, actually, isn't it?

GREG: So I've been told.

NIKKI: Oh, shut up. Is it heavy?

GREG: I guess. Maybe we should weigh it.

NIKKI: Really?

GREG: Yeah, they're very strict on that stuff.

GREG kisses NIKKI.

NIKKI: What was that for?

GREG: I'm excited! This time next week...

NIKKI: I know!

GREG: Uganda! 2K15! Don't call it a comeback!

Beat. NIKKI is uncomfortable.

You alright?

NIKKI: Yeah, fine.

GREG kisses her again.

GREG: Right. Scales.

NIKKI: What for?

GREG: To weigh the case! Do you want a drink?

NIKKI: I'm all right, thanks.

GREG exits.

The scene changes.

Just over a year ago. Consultation room at a GP surgery.

JENNIFER is there with a hot drink.

JENNIFER: Probably for the best. This Earl Grey tastes like cat sick. Take a seat.

NIKKI: Thanks.

JENNIFER: Guess you'll be wanting your results...

NIKKI: Yes, yeah. That'd be great.

JENNIFER: You were early today. You're never early.

NIKKI: Like to keep you on your toes.

JENNIFER consults some paperwork.

JENNIFER: Right, let's have a look. CD4 is steady – you're on 390. What were you / last time –

NIKKI: 364.

JENNIFER: 364. Slow progress.

NIKKI: It's OK.

JENNIFER: And viral load...
OK, your viral load's actually gone up slightly.

NIKKI: How much?

JENNIFER: You're on 240.

NIKKI: 240? Are you sure?

JENNIFER: CD4 390, viral load 240.

Beat.

NIKKI: I don't believe it.

JENNIFER: So we need to have a chat through the possible / reasons why –

NIKKI: This is bullshit.

JENNIFER: It's probably nothing to worry about.

NIKKI: It's gone up? You're seriously telling me it's gone up? Why has that happened?

JENNIFER: It could be any number of things.

NIKKI: Is it gonna get worse again? Are you gonna put me on stronger meds, 'cause the ones I'm on now / are already pretty fucking strong –

JENNIFER: Nikki, Nikki, it's all right. Calm down. There's a strong chance it's just a little blip.

NIKKI: Fuck a little blip! Fuck it! It's been eight months! You said most people get their shit together in six; you told me that. Don't tell me you didn't.

JENNIFER: Yes, I know. I know I did. But there's a reason it's 'most people' and not 'all people'.

NIKKI: It's not fair.

JENNIFER: Listen, 240 isn't bad. Remember where you were to begin with...?

NIKKI: But I don't know / how much longer–

JENNIFER: There are a few things that could be behind it. Is there any chance you could have caught an STI of some sort?

NIKKI: No!

JENNIFER: Really? 'Cause if there's any remote possibility...

NIKKI: No, there's... There's no chance.

JENNIFER: Have you been taking your meds on time? All the time? Haven't missed any doses, taken them at odd intervals...

NIKKI: No.

JENNIFER: Smoking?

NIKKI: No.

JENNIFER: Recreational drugs?

NIKKI: No! No, no, no, this is all bollocks! I haven't done anything wrong.

JENNIFER: Were you ill when we took the blood?

NIKKI: I don't know.

JENNIFER: Try and remember.

NIKKI: Well, I'd... I had a cold a week or so before, I think, but nothing serious.

JENNIFER: You'd be surprised.

Beat.

NIKKI: Fucking hell.

JENNIFER: It's all right. Viral blips happen to a lot of people.

NIKKI: It's not fair! I've been trying so hard to put this fucking virus in its place but it's one step forward, two steps back.

JENNIFER: No, it's *two* steps forward, *one* step back. You've been making great progress considering the horrible start you had. And listen: if you have a cold or anything in the future and you have a test coming up, call us and postpone it. It's only going to affect your samples and make for stressful times like this.

NIKKI: I thought today was gonna be the day.

JENNIFER: What day?

NIKKI: I was so excited, I really thought today would be the day I actually... You know, I...

JENNIFER: The day you what?

NIKKI: I thought I was gonna be undetectable.

JENNIFER: Ah.

NIKKI: It's all I've wanted to hear. For the last eight months, all I've really wanted is for you to tell me my bloody viral load is undetectable.

JENNIFER: OK, look. Your resistance tests were fine so I doubt we have a problem with the prescription. You said you were ill right before we took the blood – there's a really, really strong chance that that's what's caused this *slight* setback.

NIKKI: But –

JENNIFER: And it is only a slight setback. It's 240, not 20,000. Let's keep perspective here, yeah?

NIKKI: Yeah.

JENNIFER: Carry on taking the meds as usual. We'll book you in for another test in eight weeks' time and see how we're doing then.

NIKKI: Eight weeks?

JENNIFER: Yes, eight weeks. I'm sorry you're having a tough time of it, Nikki, I really am. But it could be a lot worse.

Beat.

NIKKI: There are people at the support group who just fly down to undetectable with no trouble whatsoever. And then they moan when their meds make them – I don't know – a bit constipated. I would *love* to be constipated; I am literally jealous of their constipation. Smug bastards.

JENNIFER: Try not to get too stressed about it. You're very tightly-wound lately. It's unnerving to be around.

NIKKI: I apologise.

JENNIFER: How are things? Generally?

NIKKI: Fine. Fine. New flatmate moving in at the weekend. You know that Benji guy?

JENNIFER: So he tells me!

NIKKI: He seems nice. Sweet.

JENNIFER: I think you'll be good for each-other.

NIKKI: I hope so.

JENNIFER: And were you planning on bringing up the new man at any point, or…?

NIKKI: The what?

JENNIFER: I saw you! Getting dropped off by a dashing gent! Who is he?

NIKKI: Oh, no. No! That's just – he's just Greg.

JENNIFER: Greg, eh?

NIKKI: It's not what it looks like. However it looks.

JENNIFER: He's got a lovely smile.

NIKKI: Oh, yeah, well – Does he? I didn't – We're not a thing, he's just a friend. A really good friend.

JENNIFER: I bet he is.

NIKKI: He is! Me and him, we're just really… Stop looking at me like that!

JENNIFER: You're blushing!

NIKKI: Because you're making me nervous! He's just a friend!

JENNIFER: I never blush when I talk about my friends.

NIKKI: Cut it out!

JENNIFER: "Oooh, me and my friend Sandra, we went for a wax yesterday…"

NIKKI: Stop it! Nothing's happening. God. He's only just broken up with someone anyway, so even if I did want to, hypothetically / speaking –

JENNIFER: Of course, hypothetically.

NIKKI: You are a nightmare!

JENNIFER: I know true love when I see it.

NIKKI: No! No, he's too good for me.

JENNIFER: Why? Because you're positive?

NIKKI: No.
Well, not *just* that… He's seen too much.

JENNIFER: What does that mean?

NIKKI: I worked with him in Uganda, that's where we met. We got quite close, actually, we really hit it off but obviously he was spoken for, so… Anyway, I started seeing this guy, this local guy who was helping us with everything. And then, as you know…

JENNIFER: Ah.

NIKKI: Yeah. And Greg was there, when things got really shit, you know. No sign of the guy who caused it, but Greg... I'm basically saying there's no state he hasn't seen me in.

JENNIFER: And is the girlfriend still on the scene, or...?

NIKKI: Is this all medically necessary?

JENNIFER shows NIKKI the contents of her mug.

JENNIFER: Look at this. All I get from the girls here is Earl Grey with milk in it. Milk! What kind of twisted freak does that? I need your gossip, Nikki. I *need* it.

NIKKI: I can tell! No, they split up before he came home. It was the distance, I think.

JENNIFER: Right.

NIKKI: When he got back I think he realised his social circle was all people he met through her; this ex. And *my* friends, they were completely useless at dealing with anything I was going through; treating me like I had the bubonic plague or something, so... I guess we've just been there for each-other. Him with his broken heart, me with...
Me with my HIV.

JENNIFER: And has he sussed you out yet?

NIKKI: For what?

JENNIFER: For being in love with him!

NIKKI: Give it a rest!

Beat.

We'll see. Anyway, he wants to go back next year. Heart set on it. And I'd love to do the same, but... I don't fancy my chances. Do you?

JENNIFER: It's definitely possible.

NIKKI: I won't get my hopes up. The company we do it with, they basically want a guarantee that my... *circumstances* aren't going to be an issue. Guess I've got a way to go before that happens.

JENNIFER: Come on. Let's go and book you another appointment, shall we?

NIKKI: OK.

JENNIFER: And let me know when you've set a date for the wedding. I need plenty of time to find the right hat.

NIKKI: Shut up!

JENNIFER exits.

The time returns to the present.

GREG's flat, as before.

Positive

GREG returns with a set of bathroom scales. NIKKI is again absorbed with the sheet of paper from earlier – the results from that appointment with JENNIFER.

GREG: Here we are.

NIKKI: Great.

GREG weighs the suitcase.

GREG: 3.2. You're fine.

NIKKI: Cool.

NIKKI screws up the paper.

GREG: What was that?

NIKKI: Old results. From last year.

GREG: Reminiscing about the good times...?

Beat.

Nikki?

NIKKI: Yep, guess so.

Beat.

GREG: What's wrong?

NIKKI: Nothing.

GREG: What's wrong?

NIKKI: Nothing!

GREG: What's wrong?

NIKKI: I said nothing!

GREG: Come on.

NIKKI: You tell me, if you're / so sure…

GREG: Nikki.

NIKKI: I'm fine!

GREG: Then why are you so… you know…

NIKKI: So what?

GREG makes a weird gesture to suggest tension.

GREG: So… *ner.* Talk to me.

Beat.

NIKKI: I'm just a bit anxious about what might happen, all right? While we're away. But it's all good, just / natural nerves…

GREG: What do you mean?

NIKKI: I mean about how long it's taken me to get everything under control, you know… The medical treatment out there, if anything were to go wrong – which I know it wouldn't, probably - but if I have another / blip or anything…

GREG: If you don't feel ready to go back…

NIKKI: I am! Of course / I'm ready.

GREG: We could put it off.

NIKKI: No! No, of course not.

GREG: I'm just saying.

NIKKI: We're not putting it off. We've waited long enough as it is.

GREG: I wouldn't mind.

NIKKI: I'm up for it! Really. I'm just… thinking aloud.

GREG: Yeah?

NIKKI: Yeah. It'll be great.

GREG: It's going to be epic. After spending a year behind a desk in the city, I can't fucking wait.

NIKKI: I bet.

Beat.

GREG: Hey.

Positive

GREG holds NIKKI tightly.

You are going to be absolutely fine.

NIKKI: I know, I know.

GREG: No, listen to me. I mean it. It's not going to be like last time. And if there are any issues, we'll handle it, you and me.

NIKKI: You shouldn't have to look / after me –

GREG: Don't, Nikki.

NIKKI: I just mean you shouldn't have to be lumbered / with it too -

GREG: If the HIV was an issue, we'd never have got together / in the first place.

NIKKI: I know, / but –

GREG: Stop it. I don't know how many times I have to say it: I love you. All of you. Positive or not.

And I'd *still* love you if you had no arms and no legs and you were deaf and blind.

NIKKI: If that happens, you are gonna be sorry you said that.

I love you too.

GREG: Good.

Beat. GREG kisses NIKKI.

Right, so the suitcase is a goer.

NIKKI: Yup.

GREG: Any luck with the old handbook?

NIKKI: No, I'm still going through that box.

NIKKI takes the suitcase off the scales and then, as GREG speaks, idly steps on them herself. Her weight alarms her. She steps off them and then stands on them again, just to make sure. She's terrified.

GREG: No worries. I might go shopping tomorrow; get some clothes to work in, stuff that won't be ruined by gallons of sweat. So while I'm out, if you think of anything we'll need... Do you want to bulk buy sunscreen here or get it out there? I guess we could do it at duty free but it's just a bit more hassle at the airport, isn't it? I've got my super-chic cagoule so I'm covered for rain, but... What do you reckon?

Beat.

Nikki?

NIKKI: Huh?

GREG: Sunscreen, what do you think?

NIKKI: Yeah, definitely.

GREG: Should we buy it at the airport? Or before, or when we're there...?

NIKKI: Whatever.

GREG: Small point. Must be time for food, I reckon!

NIKKI: Sure.

GREG: I'll raid the cupboards...

GREG makes to leave, but before he does –

NIKKI: Actually...

GREG: What?

NIKKI: I'll go buy something.

GREG: Yeah?

NIKKI: Yeah, I'll pop out now. I could use the walk.

GREG: Want me to come?

NIKKI: No, that's all right, I won't be long.

GREG: Sweet. In which case I'll put these away...

GREG picks up the scales and the suitcase.

... and I'll see you when you get back.

GREG kisses NIKKI once more and exits.

NIKKI, alone, takes out her phone and makes a call.

NIKKI: Oh, hi... just wondering, it is Mondays you're open a bit later, isn't it...? Great.

As she exits...

Dr Walsh, please. It's an emergency.

The scene changes.

Somewhere, on the same evening, OLLY is on the phone.

OLLY: An emergency, yeah. Definitely. I think. I've just been looking through one of your leaflets that I just happened to find, casually, and I was wondering if... I'm just a bit worried about my, uh, situation? If you know what I mean...?
Yeah.
Yeah.
There is no last time.
No, I mean I've never been tested.
Really?
Yeah, maybe.
How soon can I come in?
OK.
OK.
Wait, do I need to bring a parent?
Oh, OK.
Bye.

Positive

OLLY exits. The scene changes.

The same evening. NIKKI and BENJI's flat.

BENJI shows in MATT.

BENJI: Here we are! Sorry, it's hardly a mansion...

MATT: It's nice! Cosy.

BENJI: Nicely put.

MATT: I bought some good takeaway menus – I know you've probably got millions already, but these are all great. Tried and tested. And they don't take years to deliver!

BENJI: I'm easy.

MATT: Oh, and wine. I know it's a cliché to bring wine, but this stuff's amazing, so... get over it.

BENJI: Awesome. Takeaway's on me, by the way.

MATT: No way!

BENJI: Yes way! You bought dinner on Saturday.

MATT: Only 'cause you paid for all the drinks on Friday.

BENJI: And that was 'cause you paid for the cinema before that. It's my turn.

MATT: We'll see about that. You live with Greg's girlfriend, right?

BENJI: Yeah.

MATT: When's she back?

BENJI: I think she's staying at his.

MATT: Excellent.

BENJI: Why?

MATT: I don't know. Two people, few dates down, place to themselves... you tell me.

BENJI: Oh.

MATT: Yeah.

MATT kisses BENJI.

Been waiting ages to do that.

For a moment, BENJI is there in the moment with him. He nervously changes course.

BENJI: Shall we order something?

MATT: Huh?

BENJI: We should get the food in.

MATT: Er – yeah.

Positive

BENJI: What do you want?

MATT: I vote Indian, / but –

BENJI: Great. Indian it is.

Beat.

MATT: Sorry – should I not have done that?

BENJI: Indian's fine.

MATT: I meant the other thing.

BENJI: No! No, I mean you shouldn't *not* have…
                 It's fine.

MATT: Really?

BENJI: Really.

MATT: 'Cause I feel like now there's an
                 atmosphere…

BENJI: There is?

MATT: Yeah! Definitely.

BENJI: It's fine!

MATT: Is it?

BENJI: Yes!

Beat.

MATT: You really are the enigma here, aren't you?

BENJI: Am I?

MATT: Yeah. Here's me thinking I've got the whole mysterious, keeping-you-on-your-toes thing down to a tee but it's *you*, isn't it? Your mystery, my... toes.

Beat.

I shouldn't have pounced on you. Sorry. Just, it's been a couple of weeks and I / thought we were –

BENJI: It's not that I don't / think we're –

MATT: It's fine, it's fine. I've already forgotten it. It's gone, it's... where am I, who are you, etcetera...

BENJI: OK.

There's a knock at the door.

MATT: Was that the door?

BENJI: No-one buzzed up.

MATT: I'll get it. You pour us some wine.

BENJI: OK.

MATT answers an on-stage door, if there is one, or exits and is heard off.

Positive

MARGO: Surpri – !
              Oh. Hello. Do I know you?

MATT: Can I help?

MARGO: I'm looking for Benjamin Cole.

BENJI: Mum?

MARGO: Ah! Excuse me.

MARGO enters.

              Surprise!

BENJI: What's going on?

MARGO: Just thought I'd drop by!

BENJI: How did you get in?

MARGO: That smiley Polish woman let me in
              downstairs. I was a bit thrown when this
              chap answered the door; I was worried I'd
              got the wrong place!

BENJI: You found me.

MATT: Hi! I'm Matt.

MARGO: Margo! You a friend of Benjamin's?

MATT looks to BENJI for help.

MATT: Um… Something like that…?

MARGO: Oh! Say no more!

BENJI: What are you doing here, mum?

MARGO: I'd given up waiting for you to return any of my calls or messages, so I thought I'd just take my chances and come down here myself! I was going to ring ahead and check if you were free, but I had a feeling you might fob me off again.

BENJI: Well, to be / honest –

MATT: Have you come far?

MARGO: Watford Gap, dear. There or thereabouts.

BENJI: Long way to come unannounced.

MARGO: Wasn't it just? I do love a bit of cloak and dagger every now and then; spice things up a bit! Operation Benjamin, I called it.

BENJI: Actually mum, we were just about to get some dinner, so…

MARGO: So?

BENJI: So…

MATT: So you'll have to join us!

BENJI: Sorry?

MATT: She's come this far. And we're only getting a takeaway, right? Benjamin?

BENJI: She hates Indian food.

MARGO: No, I've developed quite a taste for it actually, as luck would have it. Thank you, Matt, I would love to stay.

MATT: Great.

BENJI: Great.

MATT: Where are your glasses?

BENJI indicates off-stage.

BENJI: Through there. Cupboard in the hallway, top shelf.

MATT: OK.

MATT exits.

BENJI: Mum, this isn't very appropriate.

MARGO: What else could I do? You'd basically cut me out. I had to do something.

BENJI: I've got company!

MARGO: I know. Matt seems nice. You didn't tell me you had a partner!

BENJI: Don't say it like that. We've only been seeing each-other a couple of weeks.

MARGO: That's lovely! And does he have you-know-what?

BENJI: No, he doesn't.

MARGO: Oh.

BENJI: And I haven't told him yet, so please don't say anything.

MARGO: Of course I won't! But I'm not leaving here until you and I get / a chance to –

MATT returns with glasses.

MATT: Here we are.

BENJI: Great.

MATT: Shall we order?

MARGO: Oh let's, I'm famished! I wanted desperately to stop off at a service station on the way but I can't deal with those awful slip-roads that re-join the motorway afterwards. Have you seen them, Matt? They're terrifying.

MATT: Valid fear.

BENJI: Mum, please.

MARGO: What? Just making chit-chat!

BENJI: About *roads*?

MATT: What'll it be?

MARGO: Just a mild koo-mar for me.

MATT: Sounds good to me! Benji?

BENJI: Have they got any valium?

MATT: Sorry?

BENJI: Lamb masala, please.

MATT: Shall I just grab some rice and that as well?

MARGO: Absolutely.

MATT: What's your address?

MARGO: [*To BENJI*] You're not going to let him order it, are you? He's your guest! Here, Matt, give it to him. He'll do it.

BENJI: Fine.

MATT: How kind.

BENJI takes the order and exits, shooting MARGO a look of warning as he goes.

Beat.

MARGO: So. Matt. What do you do?

MATT: I'm in the press office at Transport for London?

MARGO: Ah.

MATT: Yeah, that's most people's reaction.

MARGO: You must get quite a lot of grumbling.

MATT: Fair bit, yeah. Because obviously it's my fault someone once had to wait a few extra minutes for a train...

MARGO: Oh gosh, yes, the service is appalling, isn't it?

MATT: Er – sometimes, yeah. Yeah.

Beat.

MARGO: Do you mind my saying something?

MATT: No?

MARGO: You look quite – um – what's the word?

MATT: Uncomfortable?

MARGO: Heterosexual! You look quite heterosexual.

MATT: Oh right - ?

MARGO: Obviously I mean that as a compliment.

MATT: Obviously…

MARGO: Well, you can spot a gay from five miles away, can't you? You used to, anyway, times have changed so much.

MATT: So I hear.

MARGO: And so they should! Viva la gays!

MATT: Absolutely…

BENJI returns, to the relief of MATT.

BENJI: All done!

MARGO: I was just telling Matt he looks quite heterosexual.

MATT: I even play *sports*!

MARGO: You never! See, Benjamin, just because a man bats for the home team, doesn't mean he has to sit around listening to Britney Spears all day every day.

MATT: Britney, eh?

MARGO: Yes, what was it you once told me? There's a Britney song for / every occasion –

BENJI: For every occasion, yeah, thanks mum.

MATT: Interesting.

MARGO: Oh dear. I'm embarrassing him again.

MATT: I'm loving it.

BENJI: How about that wine?

MATT: Oh, yeah, Margo, you've got to try this. It's the best stuff ever.

MATT pours a bit of wine into one of the glasses.

MARGO: How exciting!

MATT: Proper stuff. From the depths of La France! My uncle's got a vineyard.

MARGO: He doesn't!

MATT: He does!

MARGO: Benjamin, marry into this family quick-smart!

BENJI: Mum!

MARGO: Well you can, now they've changed the gay law!

BENJI: It's been two weeks, can we not...

MATT: Here, try it.

MATT hands the glass to BENJI, who sips.

BENJI: Oh, that's good!

MATT: Good? *Good?* It's the fuck – *flipping*, it's the *flipping* best stuff ever, actually.

MATT takes the glass from BENJI and offers it to MARGO.

Margo?

MARGO: Actually dear, I don't know if I should.

MATT: Oh go on!

MARGO: No, honestly –

MATT: You were so keen a moment ago!

MARGO: Yes, I know, but actually, thinking about the drive home, I'd better not have anything.

MATT: Just a sip, then.

MARGO: No, thank you.

MATT: I promise you'll thank me for it.

MARGO: I honestly can't…

MATT: It's amazing!

MARGO: Really -

MATT: Have some!

MARGO: *No* thank you, I said no!

Beat.

MATT: Sorry... I didn't mean to...

Beat.

Did I say something?

MARGO: Benjamin?

BENJI: Mum?

Beat.

MATT: Well this just got very weird.

BENJI: Matt, would you mind going down and waiting for the curry? You were right, they said it's only gonna be a few minutes.

MATT: Sure.

BENJI: Thanks.

MATT takes BENJI's keys, downs the rest of the glass's contents and exits.

I can't believe you.

MARGO: I beg your pardon?

BENJI: Oh, don't give me that.

MARGO: I didn't... Don't just assume...

BENJI: Assume what, mum? Eh?

MARGO: All right then. I may as well just say it: I'm not comfortable sipping from the same glass you've sipped from.

BENJI: Bingo.

MARGO: I'm sorry; I'm not trying to be offensive. I'm just trying to be safe and, quite frankly, I don't think I'm being unfair. Did you see Matt? He just took a giant swig from it!

BENJI: Oh, come off it.

MARGO: Benjamin, come on. You're sick! You can't keep going around putting other people at risk! I'd hoped by now you might have learned to exercise a little caution.

BENJI: Caution?

MARGO: Yes! Caution! You should look it up. If you haven't heard of it, perhaps that explains why you've…

She stops herself.

BENJI: Wow.

MARGO: I'm sorry. I'm not articulating myself very well.

BENJI: I think your message is coming across just fine. It's not in saliva, mum. It's not the fucking Norovirus.

MARGO: All right, all right. I know that now. Please don't swear at me. How you can possibly have the nerve to stand there and shame me into feeling guilty is / quite beyond me.

BENJI: Shame you?

MARGO: Yes! Shame me! I can't do a thing right, can I? I try and I try and I try and then the tiniest thing happens and we're right back to square one.

BENJI: This is unbelievable.

MARGO: Give me some damn credit, will you? For goodness' sake, the last time I was in the loop about HIV was when Freddie Mercury died. Everyone was dropping dead from AIDS and nobody had a clue what to do about it.

BENJI: That was 20 years ago!

MARGO: I know it was, sweetheart, but try and see things from my perspective. I've spent most of my life in a village where someone from a foreign country gets everyone gossiping. And you expect me to be up to speed with things like this? Of course it doesn't help that you've completely shut me out –

BENJI: Because I know what you're like!

MARGO: That's not fair! How can I be any different from *what I'm like* unless you let me in? Your father found us dreadful old book down the library and that's all we've read. Apart from the occasional article in the Daily Mail.

BENJI: Oh, well, pardon me.

MARGO: You just can't bear to share anything, can you? You can't bear to entertain the possibility that maybe – just maybe – I might be able to help in some way. It was exactly the same when you decided to be gay. Exactly the same.

BENJI: Typical.

MARGO: What's that supposed to mean?

BENJI: Nothing.

MARGO: No, go on. Don't chicken out now you've started something. What's typical?

BENJI: This is just so you, isn't it? Every now and then you'll make this big gesture; this big effort to get to know me and act like you're cool with everything, but you're not, are you? You're not cool with anything. You're still just a small-minded, / ignorant –

MARGO: This is hardly fair!

BENJI: You're damn right, it's hardly fair, mum! It's always been like this. Like I should be grateful to you for being nice to me; like I should take your constant belittling as some kind of compliment. Like being gay is something that needs your help, or is something that I just *decided*.

You wanna know why I never call? Why I never wanna speak to you about anything important? Well maybe it's because I can't deal with how tiny and second-rate you make me feel.

MARGO: I'm sorry I didn't grow up in a world where being gay was acceptable. Or barely even legal. And I'm sorry I had the sheer audacity to be worried for you when you came out, or when you told me you'd caught this... disease. But I'm here, aren't I? I'm trying; I'm really trying to *get it*. And yet still, every time I try to talk about anything; every time I try to learn more about you and your world, I get ignored or brushed off or told to mind my own business, and it just isn't *fair*!

Beat.

I just wanted to see you, to make sure you're OK.

Are you? OK?

BENJI: I'm all right. My life's a bit of a joke: I don't sleep. My job only gets me out of the house a few hours a week. I feel like I'm walking around with some dirty secret. I've started seeing this amazing guy who'll probably run a mile as soon as he finds out. My own mother looks at me like I could drop dead at any moment. Other than that, I'm on top of the world.

Silence.

MATT enters with newly-delivered takeaway.

MATT: It's here.

BENJI: Great.

MARGO: I do love you, Benji.

MATT: Aw...

Beat.

MARGO: You know what, perhaps I should go. Look at me – interrupting your evening!

MATT: But your food's here!

BENJI's phone rings.

MARGO: That's all right. Pop it in the fridge, you can reheat it tomorrow.

BENJI answers.

BENJI: Hello?

MATT: No, don't be silly, you should stay! It's great, this place, it's really good.

BENJI: What's wrong with her?

MARGO: No, honestly. You make the most of it. I'm sorry, I barged in on your date...

MATT: Not at all! And I'm sorry about before, by the way, with the wine – I was just really keen / for you to –

MARGO: I should apologise, I don't know what was the matter with me.

MATT: That's / fine -

BENJI: Is she on her own?

MARGO and MATT become aware of BENJI's conversation.

OK. I'll come now.
Yeah, I'll make sure her boyfriend knows.
Bye.

He hangs up.

MARGO: Everything all right?

BENJI: It's Nikki, she's at the doctor's.

MATT: She OK?

Positive

BENJI: I think I should get down there.

MARGO: I'll drive you.

BENJI: It's fine, I'll take the tube.

MARGO: I said I'll drive you!

MATT: What's wrong with her?

MARGO: I'll bring the car around. Lovely to meet you, Matt.

MARGO exits.

BENJI: Mum, it's... God's sake.

MATT: What do you want me to do?

BENJI searches for his keys.

BENJI: Please – stay, eat, watch whatever you want...

MATT: I feel like there's a lot I don't know about.

BENJI: I'm sorry, I need to see to this... You're right, we'll talk later.

MATT: Is your flatmate all right?

BENJI: Yeah. I think so, she'll –
        Where did I put my keys?

MATT hands them over.

MATT: Here.

BENJI: Thanks.

MATT: Later?

BENJI: Later. I'll be as quick as I can.

MATT: I'll keep your food wrapped up.

BENJI: Thanks.

Beat. They look at each-other. This is normally where BENJI should hug or kiss MATT goodbye, but he bottles it.

Bye then.

MATT: See you.

BENJI makes to leave. Just before he does…

BENJI: You're not gonna steal anything, are you?

MATT: Only the expensive stuff.

BENJI smiles and exits. MATT realises he left his phone behind.

Oh, you –

BENJI's long gone. MATT pockets the phone.

MATT clears up some space for the food and finds a pill bottle – the same one from the end of Act One. He studies it inquisitively, then realises what it's for. For a moment he stands and thinks, then he gathers up his stuff and exits.

The scene changes.

The waiting area at a GP surgery, later the same day.

JENNIFER is talking to NIKKI, as if showing her out of her office.

JENNIFER: Well you did the right thing by coming in. Unexpected weight loss is always worth checking out, especially when you're positive.

NIKKI: It must seem pathetic.

JENNIFER: Of course it doesn't. We'll wait for the blood results before we say anything for definite but honestly, I think you're fine.

NIKKI: Yeah?

JENNIFER: Yes! As I said, it's probably just be a side effect of the new prescription. Let alone the stress you've been under. But, again, we'll wait for the test results and just make sure everything's all G.

NIKKI: All G?

JENNIFER: What? I practically invented that.

NIKKI: I can't believe I was gonna go all the way back to Africa.

JENNIFER: Was?

NIKKI: Don't ask.

BENJI enters, closely followed by GREG and MARGO.

JENNIFER: Oh – fan club's here.

NIKKI: What?

BENJI: Hey. Sorry we took so long.

NIKKI: Greg...

GREG: This isn't the shop, is it!

JENNIFER: I'd better get to my next appointment. I'll be in touch.

NIKKI: Thanks.

JENNIFER: Have we got a Mr Roberts? Mr Roberts out here at all?

BENJI: It's literally just us.

JENNIFER: Always good to check. If anyone comes in looking like they're running late, can you send them through?

BENJI: Sure.

JENNIFER exits.

NIKKI: Greg, what are you doing here?

GREG: Me? What are *you* doing here? You only popped out to buy food!

NIKKI: I just, I – I didn't wanna worry you.

GREG: So you disappeared for an hour? Well done! Smashed it!

NIKKI: It's probably nothing. I'm fine!

BENJI: Mum, maybe we should go wait in the car.

MARGO: Hmm?

BENJI: Give them some privacy.

MARGO: Privacy? In a waiting room?

BENJI: Come on.

MARGO: Odd place to have a heart-to-heart.

BENJI: Mum!

MARGO: All right, all right.

BENJI and MARGO exit.

GREG: Come on then. Talk.

Beat.

NIKKI: OK, look, you're... You're so good to me. You know, you've had to deal with a lot: looking after me while I've got my health

133

back in order, and calming me down when
I've had my little freak-outs…

GREG: And is this another one?

NIKKI: Greg –

GREG: It's nothing, how many times do I have / to
tell you –

NIKKI: Just hear me out, yeah?
Ever since everything kicked off and all the
shit hit the fan, all I've really thought
about is how much I wanna go back. You
know that, right?

GREG: Yeah.

NIKKI: But then a couple of weeks ago, when they
told me I could, I… I can't explain it. I just
had this feeling in my gut, that maybe I'd
got carried away, like I just wanted to
prove that I *could* do it, you know, not let
something stupid like this stop me…
But I'm not ready. I know it's been OK for
the last few months and it's finally settled
down, but still… here I am. Standing in the
waiting room at the doctor's because
something else has gone wrong.

GREG: What's happened? What's gone wrong?

NIKKI: It's nothing. I stood on those scales and I'd
dropped the best part of a stone. Jennifer

thinks it's just stress or a side-effect or something... But that's not the point, is it?

GREG: Nikki, it's fine – I said earlier, didn't I? I get it. If you want to stay behind, we can stay behind. Postpone it, figure something out. I don't understand / why I wasn't –

NIKKI: I know, but...

GREG: But what?

NIKKI: If I stay, I can't let you stay with me.

GREG: Why not?

NIKKI: Because I know how much you've had your heart set on going back! And I've seen you; watched you drag yourself to work in some corporate office day in, day out, and it's not you, is it? You're like me, you wanna be back out there, helping people, and I won't let you put that on hold for another six months. A year, maybe. Not for me.

GREG: But if it's what I want...

NIKKI: Greg...
It's not what I want.

GREG: So what *do* you want? You want to try long-distance? Call it a day? What?

Beat. No reply.

Right. Look, if you want me to have that conversation with you again, about me and your HIV and this weird bullshit about you 'sparing' me from it –

NIKKI: No, Greg. No. I don't. I promise.
I just feel like maybe it's best if we... If we take our separate / paths and...

GREG: I don't understand where this is coming from.

NIKKI: I don't want to upset you.

GREG: Do you not love me anymore?

NIKKI: Greg...!

GREG: Is that what you're getting at? Is that the bottom line here? Because me going away and you staying, I'm willing to fight through that, I want to make that work. But if you don't, then... Well that's that, isn't it.

Beat.

NIKKI: I guess so.

Beat.

GREG: I don't believe this. This is honestly what you want?

Beat.

          So what now?

NIKKI: You should go. You must have loads to do, for next week.

GREG: Yeah.

NIKKI: I want you to have the best time.

GREG: Yeah.

NIKKI: I'll call you tomorrow, we can sort everything out.

GREG: OK.

GREG goes to leave.

NIKKI: Greg, I… I'm sorry.

OLLY enters, and he and GREG are roughly in each-other's way.

OLLY: Oh, soz.

GREG exits. OLLY takes a seat. NIKKI crumbles. OLLY is uncomfortable.

After a long moment…

OLLY: You all right?

NIKKI: Yeah, sorry, I'm just… God, sorry…

BENJI enters and doesn't see OLLY.

BENJI: Nikki, what's going on? What's up with Greg?

NIKKI: It's fine, I – I just, sorry, I need to – I'll be right back –

NIKKI hastily exits, as if to go to a toilet to compose herself.

Beat.

OLLY smiles unconvincingly.

OLLY: Hiya.

BENJI clocks him but doesn't say anything.

Should've known I'd see *you* here.

BENJI: 'Cause I'm disgusting, right? I need to go and check on my friend –

OLLY: Wait! Wait.
I'm glad you're here. I guess I owe you an apology, don't I? For the other week?

BENJI: Do you?

OLLY: Look, OK... In the cold light of day... When all is said and done... When the dust is settled and / the only –

BENJI: Can you wrap this up?

Positive

OLLY: Maybe I over-reacted. Yeah? A bit. But I promise I'm not a bad person. I would never intentionally be a dick to anyone. We should always be kind to those less fortunate than ourselves, I know that. Like, I give all my change to homeless people. I just bought a Big Issue. In one of my seminars I sit next to this girl who's only got one eye, / bless her -

BENJI: You don't apologise a lot, do you?

OLLY: I'm sorry. OK? And anyway, you made me think about how reckless I've been in the past, and... I mean Fresher's Week... I dread to think...

BENJI: I don't need to know.

OLLY: Well the point is... I apologise.

BENJI: Thank you.

OLLY: You're welcome.

Beat.

BENJI: I really need to go / and check on my -

OLLY: You know I'm actually pretty scared about this. Testing.

BENJI: It's good to get it done.

OLLY: Never done it before.

BENJI: All the more reason to do it now.

OLLY: God, can you *imagine* if it came back positive? I don't even know what / I'd do if–

MATT enters.

MATT: Benji! There you are.

BENJI: Matt! What are you doing here?

MATT: Date not weird enough already?

OLLY: Oh, hello? *Date?* Holler!

MATT: What in God's name is that?

BENJI: That's Olly.

OLLY: Don't worry! Just a friend! Here for the big test!

MATT: Is Nikki all right?

BENJI: Uh – she will be. / It's a bit –

JENNIFER returns.

JENNIFER: Do we have a Mr Roberts yet?

OLLY: Present!

JENNIFER: Would you like to come through?

OLLY crosses himself and then makes to leave.

MATT: Quite big on sexual health, this place, isn't it?

BENJI: Sorry?

MATT: I was looking it up on the bus. Just something that struck me.

BENJI: Yeah, well, Nikki, / she's –

OLLY: Oh my God…

BENJI: Olly, leave it –

OLLY: You haven't told him either, have you?

JENNIFER: Mr Roberts -

OLLY: [*To MATT*] He's got HIV, you know. I guess he conveniently forgot to mention it. Again. Nearly gave it to me too; tried to lure me into bed.

JENNIFER: Mr Roberts!

OLLY: I'd run a mile if I were you.

JENNIFER: *Now!*

OLLY: I'm coming. Just wanted to make sure this one couldn't poison anyone else.

MATT: I know.

BENJI: What?

MATT: I don't know what it's got to do with you, but I already know.

OLLY: Oh. Well.
Good.

MATT: And just so we're on the same page, the only *poisonous* one here is you. So I suggest you back off before we have a serious problem.

OLLY is suddenly very sheepish and feeling very stupid, but trying to hide it.

OLLY: All right! Just trying to help.

JENNIFER: Come on.

MATT: And good luck with your test!

JENNIFER and OLLY exit.

BENJI: Thanks.

MATT: Please. Do I look like I'd be good in a fight?

Beat.

So it's true then, is it?

BENJI: Look, I –

MARGO enters.

MARGO: Benjamin.

BENJI: Oh for fuck's sake, what now?

MARGO: Do you know how long you're going to be?

BENJI: No, I don't.

MARGO: Only I've been waiting in the car with that chap we picked up, Nikki's partner, and he hasn't stopped crying since he came out.

BENJI: Really?

MARGO: Getting on for five minutes! He's going to drench the carpets at this rate.

BENJI: I'm just trying to talk to Matt. About everything...?

MARGO: Oh.
Oh! I see.

BENJI: Would you mind?

MARGO: Of course, yes, of course. I'll just put the radio on or something. Drown him out a bit.

BENJI: Thank you.

MARGO: [*To MATT*] I'd plan my next move very carefully if I were you, young man. You should know... I'm not above spanking.

MARGO exits, leaving a bemused MATT.

BENJI: Sorry about that.

MATT: She's the least of my worries.

BENJI: I guess Greg filled you in…?

MATT: Once. But we were both very drunk and it didn't mean anything!

BENJI: Matt!

MATT: Sorry, nervous joke.
No, Greg didn't say anything. But when I found your medication, just lying in the middle of your flat, I kind of put two and two together.

BENJI: So you came all the way here?

MATT: You left your phone.

MATT hands the phone back.

BENJI: Oh. How did you know where to go?

MATT: Looked up the number that rung you.

BENJI: Well played.

MATT: Why didn't you tell me?

BENJI: It's not the kind of thing you just blurt out, you know?

MATT: I'd rather have heard it from you than some bell-end teenager.

BENJI: I've been waiting for the right moment. I was worried about what you'd think.

Beat.

MATT: Who infected you?

BENJI: No-one important.

MATT: Are you still in touch?

BENJI: No. No, he wasn't anything serious. It was about a year and a half ago now; just meant to be a casual bit of fun, and then...

I tried to text him, call him after I found out, but I never heard anything, so... I don't know who he is, really. Or even if he knows he's positive.

Beat.

I haven't been with anyone since.

MATT: What about that guy?

BENJI: Nothing happened. A couple of weeks ago, I'd gone up to visit my mum, which I never do, and while I was there I overheard her telling her friend that she didn't think anyone would ever... That my love life was over, basically. That nobody would wanna take this on. We argued about it, and then a few days later, when I was back in London, I just thought 'fuck it'. I was sick of not having a life! So... I went to this bar, club thing. Put on a new shirt and everything! Sounds so sad.

MATT: What, going out?

BENJI: I went on my own! I guess I wanted to prove something to myself, or maybe just disappear into a crowd without feeling like I was dirtier than anyone else... some wanky shit like that. That was where I met Olly, that guy there. We went back to his, but when I told him... you can guess what happened.

Beat.

I should have told you before. I'm sorry.

MATT: Better late than never.

BENJI: Yeah.

MATT: Anyway, look, I just wanted to give you your phone back, check Nikki was all right, so... Yeah. I'm... I'm just gonna...

MATT goes to leave.

BENJI: Matt, wait –

MATT: No, Benji, / just let me...

Positive

BENJI: Please –

MATT: No, Benji / come on –

BENJI just lays all his cards on the table.

BENJI: I know how intimidating it sounds, yeah? Before I got it myself I don't even know if I would've...

But I really like you. I haven't felt this upbeat about anyone or anything in a long time. Look at me, I'm wearing good shoes, for Christ's sake! Do you know how long it's been since I've taken pride in shit like that? I think we're on to something here. Fuck it, I think I'm falling in love with you. And I know it's weird to say that out loud after two weeks, but hey! I've got nothing left to lose, so... Please.

MATT: Benji, I...

Beat.

I just really need a wee.

BENJI: What?

MATT: I'm not leaving, I'm just desperate for the loo.

BENJI: Oh!

MATT: Yeah.
Great speech, though.

BENJI: Thanks for cutting me off!

MATT: I was enjoying the ego boost!

Beat.

Is… Nikki, is she OK?

BENJI: I think she's gonna need me tonight.

MATT: That's fine. Well listen, how about you call me later and we'll talk about all this properly, yeah? Just bring me completely up to speed.

BENJI: OK.

MATT: And then maybe we can sort out another date and watch that Britney film you're so desperate to show me.

BENJI: Really?

MATT: Really. I really want to watch it.

BENJI: OK! But you should know it's called Crossroads, and me and Britney; we kind of come as a package deal.

MATT: Right.

BENJI: And the HIV, obviously –

MATT: Obviously.

BENJI: But mainly it's love me, love Britney.

MATT: Fine!

MATT kisses BENJI. This time BENJI lets himself give into it completely.

You gonna be all right?

BENJI: Yeah.

MATT: Go on. You should check on Nikki.

BENJI: OK.

MATT: I'll see you soon?

BENJI: Yeah.

MATT: Good.

BENJI: Bye.

MATT goes to leave.

MATT: And you're right, by the way. It is a bit weird to say you're falling in love with someone after two weeks, isn't it?

BENJI: I guess…

MATT: I mean obviously I'm falling in love with you too... Like, I'm going batshit crazy over here... But I'm not gonna *say* it. God!

BENJI: Go!

MATT: Bye.

BENJI: Bye.

MATT leaves.

Pause.

The scene changes.

Just over a year ago. Consultation room at a GP surgery.

JENNIFER enters. BENJI is worked up.

JENNIFER: Mr Cole. Thank you for coming in. Sorry to keep you waiting.

BENJI: It's fine. I know what you're gonna say so we don't even need to do this whole appointment.

JENNIFER: Sorry?

BENJI: I've been having these tests for years. You've never asked me to come in afterwards.

JENNIFER: Oh. Right. / Well –

BENJI: And your nurses were ridiculous on the phone, telling me my samples were being sent off to do the fucking whatever-it-is test. I know exactly what that is, you know.

JENNIFER: OK, OK. Well firstly let's calm down a bit, shall we? Maybe some deep breaths, yeah? In…

BENJI: I don't need any deep breaths, I need you to stop wasting my time!

JENNIFER: …And out. Or not, just a thought. Sit down.

BENJI: I'm good standing.

JENNIFER: I'd like you to sit down.

BENJI sits.

Mr Cole, I… Benjamin. Can I call you Benjamin?

BENJI: That's even worse. Benji.

JENNIFER: Benji. Nice name.

BENJI: Thanks.

JENNIFER: You know when I was a kid I had a hamster called Benji.

BENJI: Really?

JENNIFER: Yeah, feisty little...
No. No, I didn't. It's just something I say
to break the ice.

BENJI: Right.

Beat.

JENNIFER: Listen, Benji. You've tested positive for
HIV.

BENJI: OK.

JENNIFER: I understand it might be a difficult thing to
wrap your head around / but –

BENJI: When can I start treatment?

JENNIFER: Well... That's up for discussion, actually;
you might be able to... Are you all right?

BENJI: I'm fine.

JENNIFER: I feel like I've just told you your plane's
been delayed.

BENJI smiles unconvincingly.

It's different, isn't it? Thinking about it,
building yourself up for it, and actually
hearing it.

BENJI: A bit.

JENNIFER: Well, listen. We need to do some more tests to get a better idea of what we're dealing with. But you said so yourself; you get tested all the time. It's been caught early, that's great. That's really great.

BENJI: OK.

JENNIFER: Most people with HIV now, they live a happy and relatively hassle-free life.

BENJI: I know.

JENNIFER: All right then. And hey, you wanna know the best bit?

BENJI: What's that?

JENNIFER: You get me! We're going to have a lot of fun, I can tell.

BENJI: What?

JENNIFER: No, really, we are! I'm here, any time you need anything. I'm going to give you these leaflets… 'So You've Got HIV' type thing. I know the illustrations look like they were done on Paint by a 7-year-old but give them all a read.

JENNIFER hands BENJI some leaflets.

BENJI: Thanks.

JENNIFER: We also run support groups, 1-on-1 counselling sessions… everything. I recommend you give it all a good think-through, because they help. They really do.

BENJI: OK. Thank you.

JENNIFER: No worries. Right, well, I'll just grab one of the nurses and we'll set you up with some more appointments to decide our next move.

BENJI: OK.

JENNIFER: I'm Dr Walsh, by the way. Jennifer. Not Jenny. I hate Jenny.

BENJI: I had a hamster called Jennifer.

JENNIFER: Did you really…? Ah! See? Bantering already. I'll be right back.

JENNIFER exits.

Alone, the news begins to properly dawn on BENJI.

After a moment, there is a knock and NIKKI enters.

NIKKI: Hey, I – Oh my God, I'm so sorry, I thought Jennifer was in here…?

BENJI: It's OK. She's just popped out for a second.

NIKKI: OK. I'll wait outside. Sorry, I can't believe I just barged in, that's really bad isn't it…

BENJI: Don't worry about it.

NIKKI: I apologise.

BENJI: Honestly…

NIKKI: Oh no! You've got the Leaflets Of Doom! I'm sorry.

BENJI: Oh! Er – yeah…

NIKKI: Oh Christ, look at me, that's none of my business…

BENJI: It's OK.

NIKKI: Fucking hell, this is just… God, I'm so sorry.

BENJI: Really, / it's not –

NIKKI: I'm positive as well, you see.

BENJI: Oh, wow.

NIKKI: Yeah, I was in Uganda doing charity work. Didn't get paid, but did get HIV from banging a local!

BENJI: Oh!

NIKKI: Sorry, inappropriate… *Anyway…*

BENJI: That sounds horrible.

NIKKI:	Yeah, well, I was almost relieved actually; my first symptoms were so bad they thought I had malaria!
BENJI:	Blimey.
NIKKI:	Got medically evacuated, which is less exciting than it sounds.
BENJI:	I'm sure.
NIKKI:	But yeah... bla bla bla! Life story! Too much information!
BENJI:	It's good that you're so upbeat.
NIKKI:	Exactly. And just so you know, it's not as bad as it's cracked up to be. One of the guys from the support group has actually renamed it Happiness And Enthusiasm Vessel! You know, 'cause... HIV...

Beat.

He thinks enthusiasm starts with an I, but it...

He's a dick, to be honest, but... You get the message.

BENJI:	Yeah. Thanks.
NIKKI:	You should come! To our group. I know how it sounds, especially now you know that me and Mr Enthusiasm With An I are

156

there, but honestly, I can't recommend it enough. It's all in one of those leaflets. The orange one, I think. I did the illustrations myself!

BENJI: Yeah, thanks. I'll think about it.

NIKKI: I'm Nikki, by the way.

BENJI: Benji.

NIKKI: Cool name!
Here, give me your phone.

BENJI: You want my - ?

NIKKI: Just for a second.

BENJI: Er...

NIKKI: I'm not gonna nick it.

BENJI gives NIKKI his phone. She taps a phone number into it.

I know how scary this first bit is, so... Give me a shout, if you want to speak to someone or ask anything, or... if you just need a friend.

She hands the phone back.

BENJI: Thank you.

NIKKI: Anyway, I'll leave you in peace. Sorry again for barging in.

BENJI: It's fine.

NIKKI: And I know it sounds ridiculous, but you'll be OK.

BENJI smiles.

NIKKI exits.

The time returns to the present.

BENJI stands for another few moments, then exits.

End of play.